Cheap and Easy...
Just Like Me

Jackie Wildman Hooks

The Most Ordinary Girl in the World

*****Cover art thanks to Queenfriday Photography!
Follow her on Instagram @queenfridayphotography*

*****Title Page art thanks to Grace Hooks*

Copyright © 2023 by Jackie Wildman Hooks

To my Bears…The Grizzly, The Brown Bear, The Polar Bear, The Koala Bear (sorry…I didn't know it was a marsupial) and The Panda Bear…You are the stars in this crazy reality show called, The Hooks House. I love you with my whole life…Because my heart just isn't big enough.

To Cassell and Jody who relentlessly push me to tell my funny stories and swear I should be a stand-up comedian. Thanks for always laughing.

To Claire Bear and Tana who still make me do yoga on occasion and cover my life with essential oils and endless moments of listening over tequila or bubbly shit and bougie food that I would never make.

To Jake Jones. My work bestie. You are the fun in all my funny…the best pair of khaki slacks in my life…Linda Churchill, you raised a good one.

To Mama who has lived so much of this book alongside me and texts me every single time someone likes something I write…that's what moms do. You do it well.

To Moe. Tell me a story…And I did…And you laughed so hard. I will miss you forever.

And Finally, to my neighbors…I'm just so sorry the trashy loud family moved in next door.

Cheap and Easy Words of Wisdom...

My heart is absolutely for us Ordinary People. I am on our side. Because I am the most ordinary girl in the world. All of the folks who sit in the kitchen at night, doing mountains of dishes...or staring at dishes...who are hoping for the best. For all the people who feel guilty for not saving for kids' college educations, or for living paycheck to paycheck or for not buying organic food because it costs too much. All of us who work more than one job to make sure our people are living their best lives. And would do it all again with a smile...because we love our people. The ordinary assholes making this world grand. My favorite type of people.

For those of us with old ratty bras and holes in their underwear who break the bank to buy back to school clothes...who buy cheap shampoo and turn bottles upside down in their showers to eek out the ending until it's grocery time again...I see you. I see us. I believe we are the real mountain movers living the real lives out here...We are not influencers. Heck, we can't afford the shit they peddle. But we can laugh at our dinner tables eating hot dogs and leftovers.

I am in firm belief we are the REAL influential people. We have JOY. We have been made to feel bad or less than at times, and we are not. We are the ordinary masses who work for good all the time...who love the people right in front of us and believe beyond belief in the power of kindness and smiling at strangers. We are the ones who will do anything for our friends and neighbors and the folks planted next to us. We are the ones keeping the world spinning. And I think we often judge our own piece of life on this planet...And I'm here to tell you this:

1. Life is fucking hysterical. Keep laughing. Seriously. Just keep laughing.
2. You have bled water from a million rocks and it shows. Be proud of you.
3. You are brilliant with your cheap and easy dinners. Brilliant.
4. You're not alone if you don't have a savings account. Life happens.
5. Know your social security number. And your kids numbers too.
6. You make the world a better place for so many. Trust this.
7. Your voice matters. Trust this too.
8. You have felt less than others far too long...Stop. You're amazing.
9. Your Ordinary Life is Extraordinary.
10. You are the miracle people have been waiting for...

This book is about the simple life. Cheap and Easy...Just Like Me. This is about getting the most out of ordinary moments, and not taking yourself too seriously. I could care less about color schemes. I could care less about fad diets (although I constantly have to give up gluten because my ankles hate me). I could care less about "presentation". I could care less about what's trending in the world, and I have no clue what is cool anymore. I'm just living my life the best I can...And that seems to be pretty great most days.

I care about living my best life…And I care about YOU living your best life too. This isn't about getting rich or feeling rich or pretending you give a shit about any of the above. I can't hang with small talk. But I can hang with laughter and ordinary assholes who bring the tequila and the funny stories. These are my people. All the time.

So, this book is filled with my favorite stories. These are just stories from my ordinary life. The ones I love the most with my ordinary kids and my ordinary spouse. My ordinary dogs too. And my cheap and easy dinners…Because who can't use some real kitchen recipes...Not the bullshit ones we can't accomplish on a Wednesday in between theater and football and jobs and letting pets out to pee. This is just the wisdom in the bullshit. This is just my daily life from my journey. I believe the ordinary moments are the extraordinary moments all the time…Magic is in the daily. And that is where I live my life. And I bet it's where you live your life too…

These are my tips and tricks and my life hacks. This is my handbook and my survival guide that helps the ends meet and the bows get tied. This is how I can put my head on my pillow at night and know I made another day work. This is how I get through and get by. And this is actually what I want to share with people all of the time…There are secrets we middle aged folks have learned in need of sharing. So, get yourself a highlighter. Get yourself a bookmark. Get ready to underline and dog ear and make notes. This book is your Cheap and Easy handbook to make your life even better. I believe in you and all you are doing all the time.

And by the way, this book is meant to remind you that you are amazing. You are living your best life. You look great with messy hair and without make up and your cozy pj pants are a masterpiece. I hope this book finds you happy. Just real damn happy. Because that is where this book finds me.

Cheap and Easy Part I:
Be Your Own Entertainment

The most important piece of living the Cheap and Easy good life is: Just sit down together again and again. Forget about being perfect...be Excellent instead. Forget about pretty plates and elbows off the table...Just keep your people sitting down together as often as possible.

When Corey and I bought our first house a million and four years ago, we paid $250 for a dinner table. It is a big, teak table and it has stood the test of time. We never ate meals at it when we were younger. But we bought it. And the thought was, someday, we would eat dinner around it with our kiddos. We made a lot of parenting promises before we had kids. We were awesome parents back then...no kids...so many worthless theories. But the table. It was one of those things we just put into action...We have been sitting down to dinner at this same table (because who can afford a dinner table these days) with our children for nearly two decades...Same table. Same group of assholes gathering.

When our kids were younger, we tried really hard to have some holy agenda. We prayed before the meals. We sat until we were excused. We asked "Highs and Lows". We did Bible Studies there for a while. We played Table Topics (still totally fun). Questions on napkins. Played, "Would You Rather" ...All the things to make sure it was a wholesome table by "good people" standards. But somewhere along the way, we realized the table itself was not the miracle...the people sitting around it were the miracle...the fact we keep coming back IS the miracle...no formal agenda is needed. Just love at a table. A loud table. Room for extra chairs. Cheap and Easy dinners. Nothing else seems to matter.

If you come eat dinner at my house any day of the week, you will be smooshed into a table that easily fits 6 but doesn't fit too many more...but we pull up chairs and benches anyways. You will see zero percent of a passing food rotation and lots of grabbing and loads of talking over each other. Someone always doesn't like something. And you will hear me begging for electronics to go up (except when I'm on MY phone, of course). And you'll see kids sneaking their phones too. You quite possibly will witness an argument, hear no less than 15 cuss words, see everyone feeding the dogs under the table, laughter laughter laughter, no one having a drink because apparently no one ever remembers to pour themselves a drink, paper towels for napkins and cheap paper plates if I'm lucky. You might get to hear a pep talk. You might get to see an annoying group hug. You might get to hear a dissertation on David Bowie or politics or Pokémon or Water Polo depending on which kiddo is feeling particularly passionate. It's a literal hysterical shit show most nights. And I love it.

I would say this nightly affair is a centerpiece for my life. For my family. It is priority one. If you are home, you are eating dinner with your family. Cheap and Easy. I play referee at least once a week. And have to say, "Let the other person speak," a ton. But mostly we just laugh. Laughing is my favorite. And we have some pretty funny people in our family. I have asked my children their favorite funny stories I tell...All of these are dinner table stories so just let that sink in...I might be the worst parent ever...And you can know that if you think your life is a little trashy, mine will top it...But if you secretly love it a little on the trashy side, you are my people…Welp, come on over to my Cheap and Easy life…This is the good stuff, y'all.

Dad Shits in a Bush...

Corey and I were about 1 month into being married. We lived in Virginia Beach, VA in a cutie pie little apartment. We partied a lot. We were party people then. We are still party people for sure, however, I am old and cannot stay out till the sun comes up anymore...But in our 20's it was a different story all together.

We had gone out on a Wednesday night and tied one on...Like crazy tied one on...More drinks than humanly possible. And for some reason neither of us felt particularly horrible the next day and went out again on Thursday.

We were sitting at a huge group table...literally like 15 friends...getting dinner and drinks. But as it goes with hangovers and next day diarrhea, welp, it can hit you at the worst moments. Including large group dinners in packed bars. I watched Corey get up from the table and walk faster than usual to the bathroom which was located right next to the kitchen. I watched Corey walk immediately back to the table. Pale faced. Sweaty. Make eye contact with me, and state, "We have to go right now."

Outside we were half running to the car. And Corey let me know instantly I was driving. He was going to be in the passenger seat doing everything in his power to not let loose his bowels on the same seat. Side note, this was my first new car I had ever purchased which I would be driving my avoiding-beer-shits-newlywed-husband as fast as I could to our apartment. Second side note, it began to rain. Hard. I feel like somehow this is a metaphor for life or marriage...But who knows...maybe it's just a public service announcement for don't party too hard two nights in a row...

I am driving as fast as I can in the pouring down rain. Windshield wipers on high and still I can barely see. My husband has his feet on the dash. Sweat is pouring down his face. He is pale. There is no radio on. And he is begging out loud, over and over, "Please don't shit on Jackie's new car. Please don't shit on Jackie's new car. Please don't shit on Jackie's new car." This is his mantra. It is on endless repeat. And I, being the awesome wife I am, am laughing hysterically.

There is a break in the mantra for him to turn to me so seriously and say, "You have to get off the highway. I am going to shit myself now. Right now. Get off the fucking highway."

I can barely see between the rain and the tears from laughter rolling down my face. I cannot compose myself enough to have compassion. Corey is literally half yelling half pleading for me to get off the highway in the torrential rain and there is not one exit in sight. I am, of course, now yelling through my laughter asking him what I should do...When up ahead we see an Exit. I take it going about 155 miles per hour. We are good. All we need is a restaurant or a gas station or any place to destroy a bathroom. There is no way to make it home. He will poop in a public place...no matter how nasty...his bowels have betrayed him, and his wife is a helpless laughing mess.

We turn right. There is nothing. NOTHING. Nothing in sight. There is no empty back road either. "Don't shit in Jackie's new car..." is again playing on repeat next to me. No longer a whispered desperate cry...it is def con four…Corey is now hollering his plea over the sound of the rain. And I'm pretty sure divorce is on the table since I can't seem to stop laughing for two seconds. We drive for what seems like an eternity. Up ahead on the left is an office building with no lights on…There is no chance to poop inside…this is all that is left. Corey is going to shit on the side of a building in a thunderstorm. "I am going to shit my pants now," he said in angry shame. And I turned into the unlit parking lot on two tires. Parked near the front bushes, and watched my husband rip down his pants while he simultaneously exploded two days' worth of poor choices on the side of a building.

It's these times in a marriage you treasure forever. I made eye contact with my husband drenched in rain, shit splattering the side of a building, and he's clearly hollering to me…I roll down the window, "Turn off your fucking lights. This is humiliating enough without your lights on me." Truer words were never spoken.

I sit in my car laughing and crying and laughing some more till my head hurts. Every once in a while, over the next half hour, I would look up at the man in the bushes, hair plastered to his head wearing only a shirt at this point…pants and underwear, shoes and socks are a goner. Too much fabric blocking the massive poop flood in the rain. These are the times, clearly, that bind you.

Corey motions for me to roll down the window. "Get me something to wipe with…Anything. I need to clean myself up. This is horrible." I grab what I can find on the floorboard next to me, and run it out to the man in the bushes. "Don't look at me!" And I'm laughing again. Handing him a stack of papers. Running to get out of the wind and rain…leaving him behind as he struggled to gather an ounce of dignity through some paperwork raked over his bottom.

He finally got back in the car. Soaking pants wrapped around his waist. Never saw the rest of the clothes again. The drive home was quiet except for me trying to conceal my laughter that kept coming wave upon wave. When we pulled into our parking lot at home, Corey looked at me and said, "That was our lease agreement you know…The whole thing…name, socials, address…I wiped shit all over our lease agreement and just left it…".

So, the moral of the story is this:
Don't wipe your ass with your lease agreement…especially if it's filled out…even more so if you're going to leave it in a mountain of your own personal human shit outside an office building late at night.

Oh, and marry someone you can laugh with…and tell this story over and over for 20 years to your kiddos…It never gets old. Sorry Corey.

Jake's Favorite Cuss Word…

Back before my kids were teens, they didn't cuss. Or at least they didn't cuss around me. It's a different story today all together, they are foul mouthed idiots now, but there was a time when their mouths were somewhat innocent. "Somewhat", I guess, is the operative word.

Back in those days, every Friday evening we would meet at my house. The neighborhood moms and all of our kids. There were about 982 kids running in and out of my house, and we would all pitch in with our leftovers from the week and someone would make a Costco run for Japanese appetizers (not sure what they were called to be honest, but they were delicious and the box said Japanese on it somewhere). The kids would play. The moms would sit at my kitchen table and make drinks and laugh and laugh.

These were the good old days of living in a master planned community. Houses stacked on top of each other. Easy friendships. Hide and go seek. Dress up. The age of innocence butting up against new tweens.

One Friday night, my dear friend, Susie, grabbed my oldest Jake and brought him to the kitchen table.

"Jake. I am going to give you a free pass for you to say your favorite cuss word."
And we all laughed and waited for Jake's response. It was going to take a lot for The Bear to break.

Jake fidgeted and said he could never say it. And we all pleaded with him that he totally could say it and would never get in trouble for it. This would go on and on, back and forth for about 20 minutes. Jake stating that it was too bad of a word, and us moms telling him it could never be too bad and it was a free pass. We were all laughing. Jake was laughing. He knew the secret word he held in his heart and the suspense was too good to be true…

I had my own guesses to what it might be…The S word…The F word…Maybe he would hit hard with MFer…But as far as I knew, this was a pretty straight laced band kid who wasn't even allowed to watch SpongeBob (why this was a rule at this time in our lives I have zero clues…but it was and I stuck to it hard core).

His face was turning red. Hands in his pockets. I figured he would go low on the totem pole of cuss words since he had an audience. Maybe just say, "Asshole" and call it a day.

At this point we are all laughing, staring at the kiddo in front of us who is clearly about to let loose…

"Ok. Ok. I'll say it, but you can't get mad mom….Promise?"

"Totally promise." I mean how bad could it be? But this moment would be a game changer…an eye opener in the world of parenting and middle school mouths…This would usher in the awareness my kiddos were not near as innocent as I had made them out to be in my heart…The silence was broken by Jake's deep breath…

"Bitchassmotherfucker."

One whole mouthful of a word answered by shocked silence. And the questions we all had at that moment,

"Where in God's creation are you throwing Bitchassmotherfucker around at the age of 12? Are you in a gang? A rap star? Or possibly the class bully?" Whatever the case, all eyes were on me, and I was howling with laughter.

These are the proud parenting moments y'all. The ones that keep on giving. I just need y'all to know this word has been paraded around for years on end…Can't get enough of it to be honest. It's a good one. Hard to throw into a sentence, but always a plus when you do.

Just a reminder from the Hooks, always, go big or go home. Especially with cuss words.

The Turkey Aversion…

I am a person without allergies. It's something I'm proud of I think. I like to say often to sneezing folks everywhere that I have zero allergies. Not seasonal. Not bee stings. Not cedar fever. Nothing. But truth be told, I have something far worse. Something no human should ever be subjected to…And that, my friends, is a Turkey Aversion.

I have googled it. I have had to explain it to coworkers. I am often ashamed, and nearly alone in this nightmare. I am well aware there will never be a gigantic turkey leg waiting for me at a Renaissance Fair. I have succumbed to being a "ham girl" at every Thanksgiving/Christmas dinner. It is what it is. And y'all, it's horrible.

I had no idea about this issue before the first Christmas Corey and I spent together married. We were young. No kids. Buying way too many presents for each other and enjoying every minute of being young and in love. We spent Christmas Eve at my mom's house. The usual Christmas experience of cousins and food and her glorious Turkey. It's the best of the best. Perfectly yummy. And I love it beyond most foods in the universe. She cooks it all day long, and it is divine.

I have never been a small girl. And when good food is on the table, I'm going to eat it…and eat lots of it for that matter. I had been the one in the Christmas buffet line going back for thirds without shame, taking bites off my husband's plate and stealing turkey in the kitchen before anyone else had the chance…It was a happy, happy Christmas. No warning to what loomed ahead for all of us.

The living room was clearing out of cousins and presents, and we were still young enough to make plans with my sister to head to the local bar…The place where at Christmas time you have a literal high school reunion. It's always crowded. Always lots of hugging. And we were all in for a night of beers and reminiscing.

I remember I was wearing an Old Navy fleece shirt with an orange puffy vest over it, some low waisted jeans and I looked cute as hell. It was 1999 and we were headed to the Christmas reunion, and I could not wait! We got into my green Honda Civic two-door and headed out. The night was young, and the future was bright. But the moment we were on the road, something changed. Something changed drastically with my bowels.

My stomach became rock hard. I looked like I was about 18 months pregnant. I was bloated and bloating. My stomach was growing by the minute, and by the time we were trapped in the car it began to happen…I began silently, with a faint whoosh, emitting the worst farts known to humankind. There were tiny balloon-air-escaping squeaks here and there, but mostly it was just ninja like gas bombs going off repeatedly. Over and over the gas would build up and destroy the air. It was like nothing I had ever smelled. Like shit in a bag. Death in your nostrils. Don't dare open your mouth or it was the type to creep inside and linger. I looked at my new husband knowing full well this was an experience he hadn't planned for "in sickness and health"…This was a bloated rancid woman who had just gone from hottie to down right horrifying.

"Oh my God. I'm so sorry. I don't know what is happening to me." I looked around the car at the two people who clearly hated me.

"Jackie. Jesus. What the hell is going on with you? Are you sick?" Corey asked as he frantically rolled down the window.

"I feel fine. It's just this gas. I don't know what's happening. I don't know how to make it stop."

My sister was gagging in the back seat trapped by the two-door window option. She motioned for the gas station, and we pulled over. Jeannie jumped out of the back seat coughing and ran into the store. Corey and I stared silently at one another as I kept farting again and again. She came back with a bottle of Pepto Bismol.

"Drink this or you have to go home." I was guzzling Pepto. "Something is wrong with you. We can't take you out like this!" She was right of course but take me out they did…Bar patrons and custodial staff be damned.

We spent a night at a local bar with me crop dusting everyone. I would walk by friends from years gone past, catch up for a minute, bravely offer a hug and walk away as quickly as possible so as to crop dust without detection. I could hear people gasping and asking if something was wrong with the sewage. I couldn't use the bathroom as a cover because the long lines allowed for easy implication of my crimes against humanity. There were people all over that bar in December of '99 left shocked and appalled…breathless…thinking someone or something was having major issues…And it was me…just their old friend in town to destroy the bar with fumes like a septic mess.

It lasted 24 hours almost exactly. The bloating came throughout the night and was a constant Dutch Oven for my poor husband. There was no kissing under the mistletoe that Christmas…All Corey wanted was a separate bed and some Febreeze. My parents wouldn't even be near me. Sympathy was beyond them. There were points where I just stood outside alone and gassed the dog. It was all I could do to save my family.

It's been 23 years since I have eaten turkey except for one accidental incident at a work party when I ate some turkey chili and left as soon as I heard the host brag about the "low-fat turkey meat". There's no way I can lose a job over this issue. I haven't looked back. And I am well accustomed with a holiday ham these days too. So, I say to you, young newly weds: The road is long in marriage and often surprising. And if you think you will make it out without a tale of bodily hell at some point, welp, you are highly mistaken. I wish you the best. And keep some Pepto in the glovebox. Oh, and buy the four door. Windows. You might need them.

Two Out of Four Ain't Bad

I have four kids. Three boys and one girl. And like most good parents I have worked hard to prepare them for adulthood…Do their own laundry, Clean their own rooms, Cook, Build a resume and Vomit in the toilet. Just vomit in the toilet. It really might be the most important one of all…All your future roommates are banking on this one…trust me…college dorm roommates to spouses…they are hoping for the best in the vomit arena.

But, if I were honest with you…and future roommates and spouses to the Hooks clan…I would have to admit I'm batting 50%. Two out of four. Just half. And I'm sorry. I tried. But I have failed with two of my angels. And they just can't make it to the toilet specifically when they vomit. And I have to confess as well, it's pretty much like the Exorcist. And I have tried…And I have given lots of lessons…But my oldest and my youngest just can't seem to get their vomit in the toilet, and y'all, I am here to tell you, if you end up with them, just buy some tarps and a hazmat suit because this is going to be a crime scene if they ever get a stomach bug.

I learned about this disheartening matter when Jake was in third grade. I didn't recognize it before…maybe I considered him still "little"…maybe I didn't give Jude and Grace enough credit…but whatever the case, when he was 9 years old it hit home.

Jake came to me in the middle of the night and let me know he had thrown up. He had slept in Grace's room because he was having trouble falling asleep and she had a spare twin bed. So, after being escorted back to his bed numerous times by his tired and pregnant mother (who at this place in middle age, realizes I should have just put him in bed with me), he had gone into Grace's room to sleep. Feeling sick and his mother clearly was not listening before.

Somewhere in the night, he had gotten ill and thrown up and just come to let me know. I cleaned up the trail of vomit from Grace's spare bed to the bathroom. Cleaned up the bathroom floor and all around the toilet. I paused for a moment and wondered how much vomit could be housed inside a 9 year old body, gave him a big bowl and put him on the couch. Thinking to myself, wow, he never once hit the toilet. And went back to bed because what the hell else is there to do? The next morning I went to wake Grace up for school as Jake slept peacefully in the living room.

"I feel sticky." Grace said.

And I looked at my baby angel princess covered in dried vomit. In her hair. All over her bed. Like a Jackson Pollock painting on the wall next to her. I was shocked to my core. How in God's name she slept through this event I will never know. But what would hit home that day was simple, Jake Hooks, could not make it anywhere near a toilet while vomiting if his life depended on it…Let's just hope it never truly does. Die or vomit in the toilet? This kid is a goner for sure.

There has been a lot of direction over the past 19 years. Yes. My big baby is an adult now. I have guided him when he feels sick. I have patted his back and made sure his head was deep in the toilet when he has a tummy bug. I have yelled cuss word laden commands, maybe even employed Bitchassmotherfucker a time or two…Nothing has helped. And life gets in the way of perfection, and there are times I cannot stop what is coming and I am trapped in the hell of a man child who cannot throw up in the toilet. Near? Yes. In? No.

We were in Nashville, TN one Thanksgiving visiting my family when Jake was 16 years old and ended up eating lunch at a Chipotle. Think big burritos with lots of fixings. Jake ate an enormous meal. Chips and queso and a little guacamole to add to the flare. Washed it all down with a soda. We played card games that night and went to bed. But around 2am I awoke to my oldest son knocking at my door.

"I feel sick. I feel really sick."

And I knew what was about to happen before it happened…Jake, stumbling in his underwear, went careening into the bathroom. He was tripping and falling and heaving. Loud guttural noises over and over as he vomited everywhere except the toilet. It was like a large bull or the Minotaur had eaten too much of a burrito bowl. It was like the one kid at the slumber party who ate all the cheese balls. It was like a demon possessed beautiful blonde boy, and I was the only witness. He laid on the floor and howled, gagging again and again…Stating how sorry he was between heaves and lost dreams. He sat on the commode for a minute and threw up into the cabinet in front of him, the window beside him and every square inch of the floor. It was so loud. But don't worry, no one else woke up. Just me and Jake and his intense food poisoning to bring us together.

I let him know after a long pause in heaving, he needed to take a shower and clean himself off. Somehow he was covered in vomit too. Why make the toilet, when you can just vomit on your own chest?

He looked at me through shame and horror, "You're going to see me naked aren't you?"

"Yes. Yes I am Jake." I answered. And we both knew this night would live in family infamy and tales to tell for years to come. This is just where you are when you have to see your naked sick teenage son step over mounds of vomit to lay silently shivering inside a shower as your life now consists of cleaning wipes, large towels, tons of water and holding your breath as you wonder what the hell went wrong in your, "put your head in the toilet" lessons from years gone by…This is where I leave you.

Y'all. I can tell you we recently had the joy of a stomach bug while visiting a college together. Just the two of us. Why is it always me? And as Jake crawled to the porcelain throne, and pride swelled within my soul as I watched him expertly aim for the toilet, he somehow turned his head and threw up on the wall…behind the toilet…little ornate tiles all around. I don't know how it happened but I witnessed a near miracle and the sheer disappointment of cleaning wipes, water and towels again. I have done my best and my best wasn't good enough.

So, this really is a warning of sorts to all the future late night members of Jake's life…I cannot help you. I tried. My phone will go to voicemail. He's in your hands now. And by in your hands I mean, good luck and Godspeed. And may all your late nights with Jake be vomit free or filled with zero carpeting and lots of Clorox wipes. I'm still working on a losing battle with Josh.

It Just Happens When You're Over 40

Track is my favorite sport to watch. That and gymnastics. I sometimes wish I could run the fastest 400 ever. I can almost feel myself doing it, but alas, I have big slow legs that are less than powerful and more squishy than most. But I have been blessed with one kid who runs track, and honestly, I'm his biggest fan. I have been watching Jude run since he was in elementary school and I like to get up close and yell really loud. Like front row seat with my screaming voice saying his name over and over. It will live in my memory forever.

He does summer track. He does elite track. He does school track. He does it all. And I hate when I miss a meet. I have no shame. I don't care what anyone else thinks. That is my boy. Win or lose I am screaming for him.

"Go Jude!!!" I never know if he can actually hear me, but I'm convinced it makes some sort of difference.

I typically sit somewhere near the top of the stands while I wait to watch my athlete run for less than a minute. Track meets are LONG. They last for eternities, but races are run and won in the blink of an eye. So, when it's getting close, you don't move a muscle. You don't run to the concession stand. You don't wait in line for the restroom. You sit and hold hunger and bladders at bay often wrapped in a blanket or holding an umbrella or sweating your ass off depending on the month you're in…It's track. Long meets. Long season. Long waits. Short runs.

I was sitting with my usual group of parents. Half talking and half keeping an eye on the track. And he was up. It was his 8th grade year and he was killing it in track. I moved to the front of the stands. Weaving my way through the obstacle course of hundreds of parents in the metal stands. I was randomly in capri work out pants and a short sleeve t-shirt. It was about 20 degrees and night time so, I borrowed a blanket from a kiddo in the stands to wrap around my shoulders while I yelled my heart out. Poor kid. Never knew what she was handing over.

I had to go to the bathroom, but I didn't want to miss a thing. Now that I thought about it, I had had to go to the bathroom since I before I left school that day…But as a teacher my bladder is like a steel trap. I was good. I could hold out. I felt like I might be wrong on this one, but y'all, one race. One race. Less than a minute. Then I would walk/run to the bathroom. But I couldn't miss screaming for my Jude.

He was rounding the corner. He was out in front. I was so dang proud. He was getting closer so, I knew it was my time to kick it into gear. "Go Jude! Go Jude! You got this! Go Jude!" I was yelling. Using all the force in my entire body to scream like it was the run of a lifetime. Using that same damn muscle you use to push out your pee. And I lost control. I just plain lost control.

And it just happened. I just started peeing my pants. There was no stopping it. I mean, I'm over 40. I've had four kids. I have zero control once it begins. The floodgates were open and I was at a loss. There was a stream of pee freely running down my legs. And let me remind you, I'm down front…families behind me…the poor girl who handed me her blanket…

I was panicked and yet somehow still screaming for Jude. I'm a mom dammit. I'm a helluva multi-tasker. I can pee in public in front of the masses, and still keep my head in the race. I let the blanket slip from my shoulders like no big deal. Wrapped it stealthily around my waist as a puddle formed at my feet. And gingerly kicked puddle after puddle off the bleachers. Like a champ. Like the fucking mom champ I am.

My pants were soaked. I looked at the kid in the stands who owned that precious blanket…the only barrier between me and embarrassment…She was staring at me. I knew she knew. I fully recognized all the front row seat holders clearly hadn't missed a woman pissing her pants inches from their faces. I told that poor child I was keeping her blanket for the night. And I just kept walking. No need to chat. I smelled like urine and looked like guilt personified. I grabbed my purse and walked with solid purpose toward the field saying goodbye to no one.

I one armed hugged Jude still holding some kid's blanket around my waist like a pro and told Jude to just meet me in the car. No explanations needed. Walk with purpose. Keep conversations short. You just wet yourself in front of hundreds of people. Act like you don't notice. Acknowledge nothing. It's the way of parents everywhere.

Jude totally didn't understand why I was sitting on top of a random plastic folder with pockets and brads when he got in the car. But so goes parenting. So goes cheering for your kid when you're 40+. So goes all pride and pretense or any piece of you still feeling young. Not too many young people out there are searching for the overweight middle-aged woman in workout capris soaked with pee to make their new best friend. But there is a gang of mom's somewhere squarely over 40, who might join a support group of public accidental pee-ers if I start one someday soon.

And I'll tell you this…I would do it again…I'd just go to the bathroom first.

Big Girls and Small Cliffs

Let me start with honesty...It's really all I have left...I would like to call it a cliff for the purpose of this story...I'd like to tell you it was death defying just to make myself feel better...But, truth be told, it was a small ledge versus a big girl and a short story in self-humiliation.

My friend, Cassell, and I spent a summer taking our littlest on outdoor adventures at least once a week. She's the organizer, and she knows all the special fun spots around our town. We wear river shoes and shorts and there is always a body of water involved. We pack coolers and drag chairs along and generally have the best time. Our oldest are adult children, and our youngest are elementary aged kids...It's the bond between two parents who have kids living in different ages and stages. We work hard to give the littles the same special moments the bigs had a long time ago. It's serious business for the two of us. Mom Guilt can be crushing.

This particular summer she took me and Josh and her son, Connor, to an easy river you can walk along for the most part, but there are some swimming areas. It was beautiful. We hiked and swam while laughing and talking.

I should pause here and tell you, I have given up on caring about a lot of things. One thing in particular was bathing suits. I'm not naked, but I'm for sure wearing a bikini. I don't care how big I am. I am wearing an official two piece because I enjoy having a tan tummy and I have realized no one really cares anyways. It has been a show of solidarity with myself, and I have loved every minute of it.

And I have to add here, I was feeling really grand that wonderful summer. Wearing shorts. Rocking a bikini like the middle-aged mom I am. Thick thighs. Rolls in my belly. Rocking it like I was a super model. No cares in the world.

So, we are walking along and swimming along and I am wearing old ratty tennis shoes and a cute little bikini. The sun is out. The kids are laughing and it's like a page out of a good book. Up ahead we saw this little ledge. Kids and parents were climbing up and jumping off. It looked so fun. Heck, it was so fun. Watching them was like watching a TV show of what amazing things were about to happen in my own life! So, we swam/walked to the ledge, and Cassell and I plopped ourselves down in the shallow water near the shore to watch our boys climb and jump.

Now climbing this ledge takes some encouragement for the littles. Josh has never done this before. He is excited but nervous, and we are yelling and cheering from the water below. I'm feeling proud. Like a good mom. I'm feeling like this just might be the best summer. I'm feeling like my boy is having beautiful outdoor adventures and I'm the tan mom of the year. And maybe I should add here, I had a heightened image of myself. Maybe I should say here, I was feeling more outdoorsy than usual...I mean, I'm a writer y'all...I drink coffee...I don't CrossFit often or ever. But I was feeling strong. I was feeling lean. I was feeling invincible. Honestly, I was pretty damn mistaken in my feelings that day.

And then it happens, "Mom!!!! Come jump with me!!!! Please!!!!"

Well, shit.

This goes on for many many minutes. The loud begging. The way only little kids can when they won't give up. There is smiling and more begging and that overly ambitious feeling inside that climbing this ledge will only make an incredible day better.

And I'm wearing confidence like a strong perfume. I mean, I'm going on brisk morning walks semi regularly. I'm watching what I eat on occasion. Heck, I'm wearing a bikini and faded orange tennis shoes. This is MY summer. These are MY days. I can feel the power inside of me, and before I know it I'm swimming to the ledge. Can we call it a cliff here? Can we say the little ledge was 85 feet in the air???? It might save my pride. Just imagine a monstrous cliff. Not the tiny little ledge I side-swam, keeping my hair out of the water, up to…

I swam with all the gusto of a boxer headed into the ring certain they were headed for a knockout. Smiling up at my son waiting on the ledge, I placed my hands on the rock and went all in with the certainty of someone with upper body strength. Y'all. Nothing happened. I groped and pulled and did everything in my power. But my power was long gone…like 20 years prior… and there was nothing left, except a big girl and her big mushy bottom hanging half out of the water with on lookers getting the slow sad show of a lifetime.

"Mom? Mom? Can you pull yourself up? Are you ok?" Josh seemed so confused by his mom laying awkwardly half in the water. One leg struggling to get on the rock. Core strength proving useless. Arms like worthless muscle-less appendages. Hot Shame...the only motivator left.

I was like a beached walrus. I was like a whale trying desperately to roll upward. I couldn't find a lick of strength. I couldn't find anything to mobilize my lower half. I could hear my friend laughing on the shore. She kept trying to tell me through peals of howling laughter she wished she had a video camera for this one moment. The belly laughs were contagious, and I was now trying to throw my leg up on the world's smallest overhang. I was shaking with laughter. Ass out of the water and enormous white thighs slowly being heaved onto a low hanging rock. This was murder.

I wondered how my son felt in this moment of big girl/big dreams panic. I wondered how the athletic looking...shit, even just the semi-athletic looking families felt while they watched and waited. Did they make eye contact with each other knowing their organic food and daily exercise had avoided this fate for them?

This was the least athletic moment of my life. My 8 year old son was trying to grab my arm and pull me up, but nothing helped. I could feel the stares of families walking by...they probably cross fit together...and I was the type of person they prayed for each morning. The big mom with the pear-shaped physique slowly crushing her own self esteem on the side of a rock one summer afternoon. Bless her soul.

It took a long while...a long long while...but needless to say, I conquered the small ledge that day. I dug in deep and slung my leg up, my son and his friend pulled like they were saving me from a car fire...proud of the water rescue two young boys had accomplished. And my friend got to watch her big girl bestie make the shortest jump of her life. I've never worked so hard for so little satisfaction. Josh was less than proud. Josh just seemed thankful I was still alive since clearly the woman rolling onto the ledge showed no signs of health while she lay on the rock panting like she had run a marathon before jumping down into the water…Literally, it was like jumping off the side of a pool…no great airtime moment.

So, here's the moral I hand to you…Love yourself. Love your body. Love the shoreline if you haven't used a muscle since you were in your 30's. Know simple physics…Big bodies and small cliffs don't match as well in reality as they do in your mom dream moments. And bring a true friend who knows this only could have been better with video proof…

The Dead Deer and The Snowpocalypse

One week…one horrible week…of the winter of 2021, was brutal in Texas. Our power grid for the state could not function with all the power it needed during a massive winter storm and we had rolling blackouts for days on end. We lost power for 36 hours straight (some folks much much longer), and our well froze. We have a well and it's awesome water. However, it's electric, so, no power equals no water for us. And no power for 36 hours meant our well froze solid. We went without water for one week.

School was cancelled. Roads were closed. This is central Texas outside of Austin and we simply were not prepared for this. Most of us don't even own winter coats. We paired up who we would sleep with each night, and every bed had to have a dog in it also (we have three dogs…they are snuggly and wonderful…that part was lovely). We kept our refrigerated food on the front porch in coolers. We ran and made coffee any time the power came on and charged our phones like middle school kids at a slumber party.

It was dead quiet and boring a lot. And freezing. We were all stuck together with zero electronics so, one day, about four days in, we bundled everyone up and forced them to go sledding on our large "tubing" inner tubes (the tubes you use to float rivers on during a Texas summer). We had layers of clothes on. We had hats and gloves we dug out of a closet that were 88 sizes too small. We crammed in one car and drove about 3 miles per hour to a hill by our house. Other families were there. They were smiling. They seemed happy. They seemed like they had forgotten the electricity and heat barren snowpocalypse for a moment. And the Hooks wanted to join them…join in the fun…make a memory or two…maybe laugh in slow motion and hug a lot like a Hallmark movie.

But the Hooks are not an easy people. We are not the kind to frolic. We yelled and cussed at each other as we climbed the fence to get to the hill. There may have been some refusal. I may have almost cried giving a monologue about family togetherness and how they had all failed me. There may have been some moments of shouting, "Jesus Christ!" And other families were definitely given the opportunity to realize they had some strengths we were clearly lacking…like obedience and good will.

Nonetheless, we made it to the hill. And for about 3 minutes it was heaven. Sledding. Laughing. Snowballs. My family. So wholesome and good.

Whoosh. We pushed Joshua down the hill. The littlest Hooks who had been so cuddly and extra during our long snowed-in days. That boy sailed down the hill. Joy on his face. And went flying. Flying. No really flying. As he launched over a mound or a rock or a tree stump buried in the snow. He was sailing and it was instantly awful.

And we are laughing. Hysterically. Because we are assholes. And he is screaming. And crying. And his tube went one way while he went absolutely the other.

"Dear Jesus. Jake. Go get your brother." I said with sheer annoyance at how quick our fun ended. I must have forgotten how easily we can ruin a good time.

And Jake ran down the hill with Jude and Grace and Corey close behind. They were absolutely zero comfort to Josh who is hollering about hitting the brown rock. They have left him to fend for himself…tears streaming down his face while they examine the brown rock and systematically derail even more of our short-lived family fun.

"Holy shit. It's a deer! You ran over a dead deer! Josh! It's a dead deer!" And as the older kids gather round and laugh even louder, Josh is screaming. Maddening screams. Like a banshee in a Scooby Doo episode. Don't worry. All eyes on The Hooks.

"I killed a deer!!!!" Over and over. Echoing down the little hillside. Families staring. Families pulling their loved ones away. And my older kids now mocking him. And my husband taking pictures because we cannot find any kindness in these hearts of asshole comedians.

Before Josh could blink it was on Snap Chat. Before we could get in the car, I'd seen it on Instagram. Merciless. Appalling. But man, it was funny. They must have called him The Deerhunter for weeks on end. Tears mean nothing when your older siblings are armed with the ammo of a lifetime.

To this day, I still ask the boys to pull up the picture of Josh crying next to the dead deer. To this day, it still makes me laugh and laugh. It's one of my favorites. And I can know we might be the most horrible family in the entire world…But it is what it is…And if you can't laugh at your screaming, debacle of a white trash family as other kinder sweeter versions of togetherness gawk and point fingers…well, what the hell else is there left to do…If you can't beat them, at least post it to Snapchat…

Wear the One Piece

Many many years ago, my family visited Colorado with another family. It was a getaway hosted by a super wonderful older couple (who I am now realizing were probably about my current age). They brought us there to relax and vacation and enjoy the beautiful Colorado summer. It was perfect. More than perfect. It was downright delightful. We spent so much time together, and all our kids got along…That's a bonus.

One morning, bright and early, we were given the option to go "tubing" down the river. Now, let me say this, tubing in Texas is leisurely for the most part. As Texans, we pack a cooler, grab a waterproof stereo of some sort, ice down many beers and drinks and throw on river shoes. We tube all day and laugh and talk. We might tie our tubes together to ride the very small rapids and laugh if we tump over. Maybe you camp along the banks. Maybe you ride the river a couple of times. It's a relaxing experience. But this is not the case in Colorado. And I have learned my lesson well enough for me and every person subjected to this fresh slice of unwitting hell.

I said yes almost instantly to the river invite. I should have noted the river moving so swiftly we kept our kids away from it the day before. I should have noted there was no cooler of beer, or a stereo tied to a tube. I should have asked a few more questions. But our host assured us it was "super fun". He did this all the time with his sons. I should have noted he and his teenage sons were athletic and fit. But mostly, I should have noted when he said, and I quote, "Whatever you do don't let go of your tube. If you get sucked under just hold on to your tube and eventually it will pull you to the surface." These words felt a little ominous. A little heavy. But I brushed them off and thought of tubing a river in Texas…Bring on the beers and let the good times roll.

I was in a brown tankini when I waved goodbye to my family. Ready for this misinterpreted "fun" that lay ahead. So naive. So so so naive. Read context clues, y'all. Read them all. When someone begins a sentence about a river with, "Whatever you do…" just stay home. It's all you have left.

There was some serious foreshadowing occurring if my life was an actual novel. If there had been a narrator, he would have whispered many things to the audience watching a woman jump on a tube with the innocence of a lamb being led to slaughter. Oh, and someone would have pointed out to anyone in ear shot our guide was a liar when he used the word "fun". Unless of course, fun in your world is a beat down from a river served with a side of humiliation on a bed of "maybe-you-should-lose-some-weight-and-shave-more-often".

We grabbed our tubes and walked to the river. Myself and my friend, Krista, and the host of this tubing excursion who seemed way too confident in my abilities to save my own life if need be. I instantly regretted my decision when I jumped on my tube which felt way smaller than a tube I would pick for a girl of my size. It was like sitting in a toddler floatie to brave the open seas. We were not drifting merrily along. The water was speeding along, and I struggled to get my thighs situated as the ice-cold water pulled me at breakneck speed. I was taking this ride whether I liked it or not, and I did not like it the moment it started. But I'm a trooper, and I tried to keep smiling and force some giggles here and there…And just keep on chatting about the scenery only seen in glimpses as I raced down a river in Colorado.

Our guide was way ahead looking like a pro, my friend was close behind him and I was the big girl at the back with her heart pounding as my bottom lodged fast into the hole in the shrinky-dink tube.

"There is a small waterfall coming up. You might tump over. If you do, don't forget what I said about holding onto your tube!" He hollered from up ahead. Like it was no big deal. Like it was no big deal at all.

I watched him glide over the falls and let out a celebratory "whoop". My friend was next, and she navigated with ease. I could feel my heart exploding in my chest. And I knew before it happened, I was going under. If you are pushing 200 pounds on a tube made for small children, well, you're in over your head and dignity has left the building. Go ahead and say hello to panic and terror, your new best friends.

My weight versus the tiny tube versus the falls versus probably some formula involving mass over density squared met its maker. I was over. I was stuck. I was under in an instant. The water was pushing me down down down and I held on to that mini tube with everything inside of me. Thinking thoughts of hate and revenge for the devil of a guide disguised as a friend.

Eventually, that baby tube did what it was created to do and pulled me out of the waterfall. I was grasping the tube with one hand, my other hand flailing in the swirling water. I could not get my feet under me. I was running like a horrible cartoon character…tripping and being drug with that damn tube through the river.

I should note here the river was shallowish. I should make mention of the fact that if I stood up it was at my knees. But standing was beyond me. The river was so fast, and I was so slow…I lunged to try to get back into my tube, but all that happened was a belly flop onto the river rocks as I was now being drug scraping my thighs and stomach along the river bottom.

"You made it!" I heard up ahead. And "Fuck You," was all that came out of my mouth.

Directly in front of me was a large boulder. The river had no mercy. I was still out of my tube being careened on my belly, and I was now headed, face first toward a boulder. There was nothing I could do. And I felt the type of "oh well" give up only a mom of three toddlers can know…

"Please don't let me get knocked unconscious," was my only thought and humble prayer as my face planted firmly into the side of a very solid large rock. My tube instantly went under the boulder and I, since I am good at following directions, never let go. I went under the boulder with my tube. Face up. When I emerged about 3.2 seconds later, I had an enormous black eye and bloody scrapes from my forehead down to my collar bone. I looked like I had fought off a small street gang on the riverbanks. And I was still holding that stupid tube stuck in some reeds and I heaved myself back on board.

Y'all. Let me take a moment to tell you this was less than a minute into our adventure. Let this sink in…This is honestly the story of my life…just the universe handing out humiliation by the bucketful. There were hours to go. Hours.

I spent the next few hours in constant panic. I could not enjoy the beautiful Colorado wild with the others. I saw no animals. I felt zero percent relaxed and at one with nature. I hated everything and everyone around me, and I reminded myself time and again I was the dumbest person on the planet for believing our host when he used the word fun to describe a personal apocalypse. And hated him even more for his skinny people tube selection.

There were shouts of, "Stay to the right," and "Stay to the left," throughout the rest of this murderous killjoy of a river ride. And I would frantically obey paddling in whatever direction with the fever and skill of a fish out of water. I was no match for these moments. I was a big girl in a small tube on a raging river. This was a lesson in knowing your limits. And mine were met about 800 times while being pulled through icy Colorado waters.

We were approaching a bridge, and finally nearing the end. I could see it up ahead. And I had never been so grateful for "fun" to end.

Our guide turned to us, two women making eye contact and wondering if this was our final goodbye, and he shouted like the plane was going down, "Whatever you do, don't go under the bridge. If you do, I cannot save you."

What in the ever-loving hell did he just scream at me? The woman who gingerly threw on a brown tankini with high hopes this morning…What? What did you just say without helicopters and a lifesaving rope nearby? How in

God's creation am I supposed to maneuver this body of mine and this small inflatable tube across a river without going under the damn bridge that was approaching faster and faster.

I paddled. I kicked. I pushed myself. I worked like a woman on a mission, and I looked like a woman on the brink. I grabbed hold of the side of the riverbank and dug my fingernails in, held on for my life and jumped off my tube hurling it onto dry land. I heaved my sopping, frozen body and rolled. Rolled like my life depended on it (because dammit it did!) up onto the shore. Muddy. Humiliated. Wearing my river shoes.

I could feel it happening as I saved myself. The bottoms of my tankini gave way. As I rolled like a plus size mermaid out of the water, I felt them slip to my ankles. I stood, full frontal nudity, staring at a young fisherman enjoying his day on the river. The shock for both of us was almost too much to take.

"Oh God." Was all he said.

"I know." Was all I said in return. Defeated and half naked. Wishing I had groomed in the last 15 years.

So, friends, there are lessons here to be learned from a woman and a tankini and a small tube on a river. Most importantly, wear the one piece. Wear the flipping one piece. Big girls don't fit in small inner tubes…And shocking full-frontal nudity from a woman who looks like she was in a minor car accident is just less than hot. My condolences to the young fisherman, wherever you are, may the memory of my 1970's era nakedness not scar you for eternity.

The Surprise

We didn't know Grace was afraid of needles. It seems like we should've known before she was 13 years old, but, seriously, I had no clue. Maybe I was always taking four kids to the pediatrician at the same time for well child checks...maybe it was still the little kid age where they just give you shots while someone is kind of "securing" you...I'm not sure...But all I know is the summer when Grace was 13 it became abundantly apparent that Grace did NOT like needles of any kind. Not that anyone really does like needles...But she has a phobia of catastrophic proportions and getting in the way of it is costly. She WILL hit you. She will completely swat at your face. I've seen it firsthand.

We discovered her phobia during a regular well child checkup. It was Jake and Grace and of course myself. Grace at some point realized she had to get shots that day...And in that moment Grace got super pale. SUPER pale. And I'm watching my daughter look like she is simultaneously going to pass out and murder everyone...I've never seen a look like hers in that moment, full on creepy serial killer and determined teen combined with panic...and I knew shit was about to get real.

It ended up taking Jake and I and a ton of convincing and a touch of restraining his younger sister for the shots to happen. Grace hit a nurse. Just full on hit a nurse. And I knew this was more than a fear. This was fight or flight. I have never apologized so much to an entire staff before...Just kept saying over and over, "I am sooooooo sorry. My daughter. She clearly has a phobia. She wasn't meaning to hit you when she clearly meant to hit you."

This was on repeat. After the shots were finally administered, the same nurse came back in to tell us Grace needed blood work and I thought we were all going to set the place on fire.

We went home and I told Grace it would be YEARS before she needed a shot again. I was proud. The drama was over. The assault was minor. And I finished my day with a smidge of "job well done" because Jake and I had pulled off a minor miracle that day. I could build up my courage to torture an unwitting medical staff in the years to come…but not for YEARS…We had made it.

But life in The Hooks House is never without divine comedy. And just two weeks later we would take a stroll back into the pits of medical staff meets full on phobia hell when Grace sliced her thumb open and needed stitches.

The scream came out of nowhere and woke me up from my daily Covid-Summer nap in my grey armchair. Grace came walking into the back room of our house holding a towel to her thumb. Blood was everywhere. And she was in pain. She was shaking and crying. I told her I needed to look at it, and with one look I knew, we were getting stitches. And stitches involve needles…oh and shots to numb the wound. I was absolutely screwed at this point. And I knew it.

"You're going to need stitches. We are leaving right now. Let's go. And what the hell were you doing?" I said as I was grabbing my purse and all of my mom courage to go do things I was never trained to do with people who do not want to do them (this is all of parenting really).

"I was opening the surprise you got me. And I grabbed my knife. And it sliced my thumb open." Her knife. The one from years ago in Girl Scouts. Who knew she still had it? And had it within arms reach. Wow. I mean, way to hang on to a knife I thought was lost forever. And way to kind of teach knife skills Girl Scout troop of the past.

So, let's back up. The fact is, I had bought Grace a surprise. And it was Covid-Summer and Amazon was our only friend left. And we shopped. I can't even remember what the surprise was, but I had told her the surprise was coming, and it was something to look forward to…Also, and at the same time, I had ordered myself a scale because all the Covid bread baking and having daily happy hours in my backyard had added some serious pounds to my seriously already portly package. A scale was my gift to me to try to get myself back in line and away from all the late night Tiger King eating frenzies.

Back to the action…

We are driving to the doctor. Grace is pale and sobbing and terrified.

"Are they going to give me stitches?" She is asking me through tears.

"Yes." I can't lie to her.

"Are they going to give me a shot?"

"Yes." And she is screaming and crying and I'm crying and driving 982 miles an hour to get to a doctor who is going to probably get punched in the face. I'm simultaneously having that moment of, "Why is this always me???" The parenting question one parent is always going to ask forever.

We are silent now except for Grace's sobs. I have my hand on her arm as I drive. I'm just so sorry this is happening.

She takes a deep breath, "Do you know what the worst part is? Do you?" She's really almost shouting at me. She sounds just plain broken. And I hate that she has to live in the anticipation of her phobia staring down the barrel of a lidocaine gun. Because clearly…clearly…there could be nothing worse in the universe than what we are currently driving toward.

"Honey. What is the worst part?" And I'm crying again. Wishing I could take it all away. Hating knives and surprise packages and shots.

"You!!! I was opening my surprise from you. And it was a SCALE. You bought me a SCALE as a surprise!!!!! THAT IS THE WORST PART OF THIS WHOLE THING MOOOOOMMMMMMM!!!!!!"

Y'all. Sometimes in life there is a package mix-up of epic proportions. One that can cause pain and injury and even shots…but not the good tequila kind…or maybe those come later. This is a public service announcement to all the chubby parents in the world: If you buy the scale at the same time as buying a surprise for your child…make sure the right package gets to their room. Trust me. Open the package and THEN give the present.

I'm sorry, Grace. For the stitches. For the momentary belief your mom would purchase you a scale as a surprise and talk about it all week long and hype it up like you needed the scale more than anything.

And I'm sorry medical staff from the Summer of 2020. We assaulted you twice. Twice in two weeks. Like hands on your face and lots of swatting. May you take to the grave the things you heard the day Grace Hooks faced down needles at your expense.

But This Dog Can…

Jude is one of the sweetest souls I have ever met. Always has been. He is one of those kids who could make friends at the park out of thin air. Always amazed me. And he loves everyone and everything…Just a plain joy finder type of person.

When Jude was in 2nd grade, we did Vacation Bible School at a local church. And Jude loved every piece of it. He loved the songs. The hand motions. The games. The crafts. Everything. He was taken in by the whole experience. But his favorite part was the morning opening…When everyone was together. Everyone did synchronized dances and songs and yelled chants. Lovely 2nd grade experience for my Jude. But the best part was the dog.

You see, each morning there was a skit that took place. This skit involved a dog. And an adult would sit up on stage with a microphone in hand asking the dog questions. The adult would then move the microphone close to the dog's mouth and someone in a sound booth somewhere would answer as if the dog was talking. Simple.

There were no crazy special effects. The dog's mouth wasn't even moving. Just a super obedient, fluffy yellow lab sitting on stage while someone pretended to interview him. Cute bit. Not super impressive. A supposed talking dog. The kids saw right through it.

But Jude. Jude LOVED it. He talked about it non-stop. The talking dog. And he would laugh about the little jokes the dog would tell, or his answers to questions. He loved beyond measure the talking dog from morning opening at Vacation Bible School.

It seemed even his younger sibling, Grace, noticed that there are no such thing as talking dogs, and we soon began to wonder if Jude truly knew that this dog could not actually talk. Corey and I discussed it, and I decided I would just talk to him about it…halfway feeling like an asshole because I might burst this little boy's bubble in regard to talking dogs. But he was 8, and there was no way he really was falling for this bit.

So, on the drive home from the very last day of Vacation Bible School, I asked my Jude, "Hey, Doodle (his nickname since forever), you DO know that dogs can't talk, right?"

And he laughed and laughed and laughed. And he finally said, "OF COURSE I know that dogs can't talk!"

And I felt this weird little sigh of relief because at least, if anything, Jude knew dogs can't actually talk.

"But Mommy," I heard from the backseat, "That dog from VBS…HE CAN!"

Yep. That's my Doodle. Found the one talking dog in the Universe in Katy, Texas circa 2011. And this is why he is the most lovable kid…Certain he had found the one…

And She's Down

If you are a high school teacher, you know fights will randomly break out on occasion. You know also, not to interfere if you are a middle-aged woman. Let me add to that if you are a middle-aged woman in Birkenstocks and a long orange and white sundress and throw on a denim jacket for cuteness sake...Stay far far away from fights. You get others. You call for help. Maybe you own a whistle. I don't know. But, whatever you do, you don't step in...It is catastrophic for your pride if you do...Trust me.

One lovely day I got all cute to go to work. It was still Summer in Texas, and I wore the cutest orange and white long dress to school. Threw on my Birkenstocks because it is summer and they are comfy, donned my denim jacket and went to work. Spent the morning thinking I was adorable and loved all the compliments I got from co-workers. And let me add here what you already know, I am not an athlete. Never was. I don't move quickly...never have. I have a big mom bottom and thick thighs and a tummy that a denim jacket can help to hide a touch. I'm ok with this...I know my limits...I've learned my limits time and again.

Outside my room, during passing period, a fight broke out. Two guys, neither of them very large were hell bent on fighting in the hall. I called for help and waited a minute. I know my role. Holler and wait. Get on the walkie talkie and give the location. But on this particular day, my friend and fellow middle-aged mom, got caught in the crossfire. She was in there by herself, and I knew, beyond any reason, I was going to have to go in...I was going to have to go be part of the action. And the knowledge that went through my head right before stepping into the throng of students watching and videoing was simple, "Dammit to hell...I am going to end up on Tik Tok..."

The fight would have ended quickly. It seemed to be shutting down. But this one little guy kept running back into the mix...He kept getting out of the arms of his buddies trying to stop him and running back for another punch. Time in fight break ups seems to slow to a crawl. And it feels like you've been in the ring for hours. Giving the students around pure Snap Chat joy as you move to break up the fight and holler for help in your dress and sandals. You cannot look cool. You cannot look agile. You can only look like an idiot shouting and saying the same old same old, "Can you guys stop? This is silly..." And words like "silly" sound exactly as you imagine them.

I made eye contact with my son, Jude, who was there in the crowd. Half to say, "I'm ok" and half to say, "Please forgive me for the humiliation your mom is causing you and the days upon days of video footage you will see of me in action" ...Sigh.

Security came. A coach got involved to help. The Assistant Principals were there, and it was over. The audience had grown to concert proportions with phones recording every move. But the little guy was not done...This fight apparently meant everything to him. And for one last moment he made a run for it. And my foot. My big old Hobbit sized foot...it just got caught.

I tried to move. But I was tangled in the coach's feet. Couldn't pivot. Couldn't turn. I was going down. And down I went. To the bottom of a pile of two kids fighting and one coach and a couple of bystanders. Just slipped right on down. In my dress. One sandal now gone. My jacket feeling like a weighted blanket of shame.

But don't worry. I couldn't get my foot out. And I lay there on my back. While other middle-aged friends tried to lift me at the armpits. It was no easy feat. Rocking myself to my side. Doing a little roll. Trying to find my sandal. Sweaty like a woman who went to do a sit up and forgot that was way over her head. Zero stomach muscles here. And it showed. It was like a slow-motion horror film of my life failures...Clearly, I don't work out students. You can see it when I roll to my side to brace myself to get up from the floor. Did you get that on tape? Good. I will see myself later on your Snap Chat stories.

My husband saw the footage later that day at the high school where he teaches. My son in college saw it on Snap Chat. My daughter watched it over and over in her Art class that afternoon. My friends saw it when their kids came home to show what happened to Mrs. Hooks. Heck, I watched it at the dinner table with my whole family. Several times. I mean, what the hell. A woman lost her footing and went all the way to the floor...All the way down...Lost a shoe and the last shred of her pride somewhere on the ground of a high school hallway.

So, let me give you a pointer...Stay out. Stay out of the hallway/schoolyard/bike racks/bus lane fighting...We are not your go to people for fight break ups. Remember this in life...Remember it especially when you wear a dress and sandals. This is non-negotiable forever and ever. And it will live on...don't worry...in social media infamy...And on random occasions throughout your teaching career some kid will say, "Hey...I saw a video of you laying on the floor in the hall without a shoe…Are you ok?"

The Axolotl King

Josh is obsessed with a few things in life. Fortnite. Axolotls. And pretty much anything his older siblings say or do. And there is a significant age gap. Currently we have a Freshman in college, Senior in High School, Sophomore in High School and a Fourth Grader. It gets a little wonky in parenting. It gets a little wonky watching TV or having friends over. Or raising a kiddo who has lived his life with teens. His very best friend has the same situation so that helps a ton. And I have to find moms and dads who have surprise babies later in life so we can "get" each other. After you have made it through middle school three times and high school multiple times, there is a lot you just don't give a shit about…plain and simple.

So, I forget things about parenting younger kids too. Like, maybe check their Fortnite handles…I mean, we have friends who don't let their kids play Fortnite so there is that guilt already to deal with…But the handle…the name they choose to play under…check it…Trust me on this one.

Here is a little truth, I am really bad about checking Josh's games and messages and such. I was much more on the ball with the other three. I had big time rules about watching shows and playing video games and screen time…I was such a good mom in my younger days. Josh is one loved kiddo, but when you are dealing with a whole mess of crazy real young adult problems, welp, you forget to say things like, "You need to ask me before you choose your Fortnite name" or "Make sure your Fortnite name isn't crazy inappropriate because that is unbearably embarrassing knowing other parents see it…" Those things. I forget THOSE things.

This past summer…at the very end of the summer, mind you…Jude was standing in the living room watching Josh play game number 982 of Fortnite. He's really good by the way. And Jude turns around and looks at me with the disappointment only an older child can display when he is judging your parenting of a younger child.

"Mom. Mom. Do you KNOW what Josh's Fortnite name is????"

And I honestly thought about saying, "Of course I do." But quickly chose against the lie because either way I was doomed at this point.

"I sure don't, and I am betting that I am going to wish I did about 3 months ago…What is it Jude???"

"Mom. It's AxolotlKing…

Let's stop here. For one brief moment I felt really good. Axolotls. Adorable Mexican salamanders. I even think they're endangered. And Josh loves them. And I love that. He has a shirt and a hat with an Axolotl on it. For one itty bitty piece of time, I thought…yep…that kid loves an Axolotl…but the punch line was coming quick…

"Mom. It's AxolotlKing69420."

Now. If you're a really good person…like my mom, she's real sweet…just skip on…this tale means nothing to you except salamanders and random numbers. Save yourself.

BUT, if you are like me and clearly the rest of my family, you felt the enormous gravity of, "Oh shit..." in this moment. My son had pledged his allegiance at the dear age of 9, as the King of the Axolotls and a horrible sexual position and throw in the universal time to smoke weed. And he had had this Fortnite name all summer...popping up on Nintendo devices everywhere...to shocked parents and older siblings who I'm certain wondered what horrible parents allowed such things...

Josh was screaming, "What did I say? What did I say? What did I do? Y'all say those numbers all the time!!!" He said looking accusingly at Jude...And this was true. I cannot tell you the number of times in the last few years I have heard teens spewing out these two numbers as the butt of jokes or to be ridiculous and laugh and laugh. Teens. 69 and 420. They have not one care in the world that a 9-year-old might be present. Soaking up every last "silly" number they have to throw out.

And here I stood in the kitchen. With yet another parenting fail. With a little boy who thought he had the world's coolest Fortnite handle and a group of older siblings who had now gathered and were laughing hysterically while Josh begged to know what it meant...Y'all. I am just dead always.

Learn from my mishaps please. The kid had to pay $10 to change his name to something more appropriate. The older kids got lots of, "Y'all are horrible" and some mom eyes glaring at them. But just in case you were wondering if we are better for this...guess again...I am hoping someday it will be The Hooks Family t-shirt of choice, team name at a trivia night, tag line for a million Hooks Family inside jokes...We are just a band of assholes living life together over here. Feel good about your parenting today…You can always bet that mine is far worse.

The Adobe House Project

I think it's a national assignment handed out to fourth graders. Maybe it's global. I'm not certain, but I think universally, fourth graders are being murdered by their parents regarding a damn fourth grade project covering an indigenous people and their historic housing. Usually, a tee pee or an adobe house. And the kicker across the board...from sea to shining sea...is the fact that you must use natural items to build it...Let me say that again, you must use natural items to build it. Oh, and this project must be child made...proof is in the outcome...this must be made by the child's hands...which is on the paperwork and the email and the side eye from the teacher who knows...This is definitely going to be a family affair. This is going to be a late-night-weekend-consuming-morning-of-frenzy-of-hate-and-loathing-across-the-board-for-the -whole-damn-family.

We all play the game titled, "My Child Made This with His/Her Own Precious Hands and Independent Thoughts and Went to Walmart at Midnight to Find Hot Glue Sticks and Tiny Dowel Rods...Kid Drove Himself...Amazing Project".

This project is a lovely thought. And when the paper comes home giving you two weeks to put said project together, with 87 directions and a graph like rubric, and grades laid out ranging from failing to passing with an A+++...you pause and think, in the way only an overzealous mom or dad can when reading a very elaborate project description, "We will start this tomorrow. Heck. We will start this right now. Make a master plan. A timeline of duties. A day for gathering supplies. A day for research. We will find authentic items not from Walmart.

My child and I will grow closer. We will laugh and cuddle and feel the pride of coming together to build a tiny village or tee pee or adobe house. We will make eye contact across sticks and muslin and paints and hot glue and small rocks from the yard and faux bodies of water. This will be magic. I can't wait to dig in. This will be the best project our school has ever seen. I've lived through 47 grueling years of life. I survived a tornado once. This is a piece of fourth grade cake..."

Wrong. Wrong. Wrong.

This is a fresh slice of hell.

Josh brought home his Historical Homes project sometime in October. And to be honest, just enough time had passed between the last project for Grace and this new project for Josh. I felt fresh. I felt ready. I felt certain I needed to hand this off to Corey, and immediately made that choice. Walking away. Feeling good. And knowing, he was much better suited to grapple with this type of thing than I ever would be...Baton handed. Two boys (Corey and Josh) are going to do one helluva project.

We talked here and there over the following two-week period. Josh and I touched base on occasion with me reminding him the deadline was coming. There was an afternoon when we collected some sticks from the yard and made a list of all the things we needed. I reminded Corey a bunch about the impending due date. Subsequently, Josh and Corey picked a Friday night to gather everything together and begin the work (they would be the only two home...perfect time to officially begin...Four days before the due date).

But those two watched a movie instead. Had a great time. Snuggled on the couch. And the time was ticking. And I was feeling frantic. But only in that awesome partner way of barking the same deadline over and over. Saturday came and went. It was now Sunday. And the weight of the early American world was on our shoulders. And now we would do what parents all across the country would do: We would scramble. And we would fight. Oh yes. We would fight like our life depended on this...

We were instantly making a list. A real list and I was running to Walmart. Hot glue sticks. It's all we needed. I would go to Walmart at least three more times before the day was complete. We found paints. Used a large knife to cut sticks to the right size. Destroyed a stuffed animal to make pelts. Cut up an old T-shirt of Corey's to make the tee pee covering, and Corey wore the shirt the rest of the day...The tiniest crop top became his Historical House Uniform...A symbol of our utter chaotic desperation.

We were two parents who hated each other. The blame was thick that Sunday. And we laid it out any opportunity we got...We reminded each other of a million past failures of projects gone by...spoke of laziness and lost chances...gave each other the silent treatment whilst painting a river...using every cuss word available while burning the living daylights out of our hands with fucking hot glue. It was a nightmare. And we were in it. Together. For better or worse. And y'all, this was the "worse" they mention at your wedding. I am certain elderly couples silently pray as newlyweds kiss, "Dear Jesus and Mary and Joseph, Let them withstand the Fourth Grade Indigenous People Historical Housing Project. Amen."

The Hooks are not a calm people. And the moment that sent us spiraling came at about 5pm. Re-reading the rubric which hadn't been looked at once in the last two weeks prior, we realized Josh's house had to match the paper draft he had turned in earlier. Y'all. It was no tee pee. It was an adobe house. With walls painted red, yellow and black. A freakin' table was in the middle. Two beds. And we came undone. We simply came undone.

This project would find us fighting in the front yard. As a whole family. Collecting more sticks and rocks. Yelling while neighbors watched, and healthy families took an evening stroll. Two adults and their children picking up sticks and comparing sizes, yelling about who had failed the entire family by not reading a damn rubric or the fine print…What the hell were we going to do? I stood in the front yard googling "How to Make Salt Dough" telling Corey in no quiet voice that this was bullshit. And smiling and waving at the neighbor's dog while they wondered why my husband was in a crop top and my son was crying. A solid nod to the trashy family who had moved next door.

I was up to my elbows in salt dough. Corey had dug boxes out of the recycle bin and fashioned an adobe house frame like no other. Josh made a ladder and we let him use the hot glue gun because rules for 9-year-olds be damned. Caution was to the wind. Grace walked through the kitchen turned laboratory and made one off hand comment about the shaky structure and we pounced on her like a pack of wolves. Clearly this was a positive environment. Clearly.

As night was falling, it became clear we needed a box lid to place the 500-pound wet, adobe salt dough house to let our exhausted 4th grader carry proudly inside for the judgement of teachers everywhere. Corey and I were whisper yelling at each other about how to get a box lid. And at one point he suggested I drive to the high school and get one from the teacher work room always littered with copy paper box tops. When I carelessly asked if he wanted me to go "NOW", he told me he could always just walk to Austin where he teaches since his car was in the shop…And I stood in silence…working not to murder him…end our marriage…crush the adobe house with my fists…I silently walked to my car…the last leg of a journey…I was a warrior at this point…bloodied by this battle…but still breathing.

We got it all together. Got the paint done on Monday. Made notecards describing it all, telling the story of an indigenous people group who had no idea the hell their housing choice would make for a family in 2022. We must have said 982 times, "You better get a 100." Because that grade belonged to all of us…all of us…If we failed, we failed together.

And maybe that's the point. The project does not bring you together. It tears you apart. From the inside out. But the failure binds you. The group family failure binds you together forever. When a family fails together, they are bonded for life. Maybe this is what it's all about…Maybe it's this great scientific cosmic psychiatric process of failure…and parent strength…allowing fourth graders to see inside the workings of adult perfectionism and slow death…I have no advice to give…Just buy a project online…pay a friend…this is not for the faint of heart…we may have to start counseling. And Corey might still be wearing that crop top.

Red Paint and Toddlers

Prince. So many songs make the soundtrack of my life. Who doesn't want to party like it's 1999? And dream of being hot enough to rock a thrift store Raspberry Beret…Or maybe dance in the Purple Rain…or recite, "Dearly Beloved, we are gathered here today to endure this thing called life…" like only a group of partying people can when "Let's Go Crazy" comes on…It's Prince. And he inspired a generation with all of his flamboyance and guitar. He was gone. Gone too soon. And a group of us middle aged moms threw on some purple and went out to celebrate his legacy.

Corey stayed home. He was in charge of one thing: The two-year-old. We were living in a rent house in Katy, TX. And if you have ever lived in a rent house, you know the daily stress of don't mess shit up that cannot be easily repaired. Don't ruin the floors, the doors, the windows, the patio…whatever it is…But for God's Sake, whatever you do, DON'T ruin the carpet.

We had a run in with carpet annihilation a few years back when I spilled an entire Venti Pumpkin Spice Latte in a closet. We had to replace the carpet. It could not be salvaged. It could not be saved. And we had promptly purchased a steam cleaner after this event to hopefully save us and our deposit in the future.

We had taken our friend's golf cart out to the bars close to our lovely master planned community. Literally, like 5 of us, crammed on a golf cart with a stereo blaring Prince music, dressed in purple, already half lit headed out for a night on the town. We were making friends everywhere we went, and the other patrons had the same idea in mind. Prince music poured out of the sound system at the bar too, and we all just kept buying drinks and singing along. We were having the time of our lives the way only a group of moms let loose can...caution to the wind...keep the shots coming...laughter galore and telling all the younger girls in the bathroom line how gorgeous they are...It's what women do.

All of a sudden, my phone started blowing up with texts. The dread I felt before I read them was real. It's the dread of a woman who knows this can only mean one thing: Something has gone terribly, horribly wrong at home. I paused. I took a deep breath. And checked my phone.

There was a picture of Josh's room covered...I mean completely covered...in bright red paint. The floor, his bed, the walls, the shelves, large puddles of bright red paint everywhere. I had never seen such a thing. I had never seen so much paint. I could never have guessed this was going to happen...It was insane to be viewing. It was insane to be standing in a bar wondering what in the ever-living fuck had happened at home. And what in the actual fuck was I going to do about it...It looked like a school project massacre. And there was Josh in the picture too...Bright red from head to toe.

"Oh my God! What the hell happened?"

"He was upstairs with Annabelle and Grace. They were watching him."

But they were in second grade. And they clearly were NOT watching him.

"Get towels. I'm coming home."

I got a ride on the golf cart home. Terrified of the mess awaiting me. Knowing I was going to be of little to no use with the exception of one trait every mom possesses…Just start starting. Just start starting to clean that mess. Don't think. Clean. Don't wonder what to do. Just start doing something.

I arrived to my shell-shocked husband who was definitely angry with me for some reason…wondering why I had given paint to a two year old.

"Why would you give a two-year-old an enormous bottle of red paint????" He asked before my feet hit the driveway.

I didn't answer. This was a question for no one. It was a question to find someone somewhere to point a finger…a tactic used in marriage crisis of paint and epic proportions through the centuries. I am sure there are tales being passed around in the afterlife of moments of paint or dye or berries or something from days gone by with moms knowing they never handed their pre-historic two-year-olds buckets of dye worthy berries…But they, I'm certain, did what I did that night…just started cleaning up. It's what we have. It's in our DNA. We just start doing something to fix the madness.

There was water and soap and cleaning supplies like I had never seen before in my life. There was a little boy in a bathtub who had no reverence for what he had caused. He was proud. So proud of the work he had accomplished in mere moments. There were large beach towels that would never see the light of day again, and toys being thrown in the trash because who cares anymore for beloved toys when they are soaked in red paint and the blame of two parents and two second grade girls who needed someone else to be responsible. It was insanity that night. I actually hated myself for having a good time because cleaning up an art supply massacre at 11pm felt like a hell I had never known before…and I haven't known since.

There were moments of solidarity where Corey and I talked about the amazing team we were…There were moments of near divorce when a fresh puddle of paint was found under Josh's bed…There were moments full of snacks and quiet with two adults at a breaking point they had not counted on…And the lingering fear was always there: Was our damn rental deposit gone for good? Renting. It feels awesome when the garbage disposal breaks, and you make one phone call to a landlord who saves the day with zero dollars involved…it feels like a hellish nightmare when a two-year-olddiscovers the art closet in the hallway and makes a mockery of easy pour lids.

We were a family on the edge that night, and every new person who walked in our house was taken to see the crime scene and shown pictures from iPhones that would become monuments to the worst spill of red paint this side of an elementary school classroom. We were in deep. Wondering if we would make it out alive.

Our steam cleaner worked overtime. I'm certain it was not created for a mess of this size. But we used it and re-used it till the evidence was a mere whisper…a hint of pink in one area about the size of a small body. We eventually called in a professional. It was all that was left. Fork over the money and admit defeat. Move bottles of paint everywhere to the tops of closets and forbid climbing. Just forbid the whole practice. And burn all the ladders and step ladders because they are clearly part of the problem. Enact police rule in the area of art projects…small dollops of paint are all you can use with extreme supervision and a side of shame and blame if you make one false move. No Jackson Pollocks allowed in this house. Save your artistic genius for your own home…We will only be painting by numbers here…or using pencil drawings as our medium of choice. Expression is out. Especially if that expression must be painted. The risk was too high. We had seen firsthand what inspiration can do to the carpet.

The truth of the matter is marriage is fragile. You never know where the weak spots are, and what mole hills might become mountains at 11pm on a Saturday. And red paint is one. This is really just a public service announcement to parents of young kids or newlyweds or grandparents babysitting a crew of experimental abstract free form artists…Put the paint up high. Lock it in a box if needed. Or forbid it. That's an option too. But whatever you do, don't have a night of fun if red paint is somewhere in the house. Karma is a true bitch. And I am positive I was paying the price…or living through some generational curse…We lost the deposit. The whole damn thing…And if you wondered if we have matured enough to quit blaming each other for this one, don't worry, we totally haven't. The picture of the painted room popped up on a timeline just about a month ago…The grudge is holding strong.

Car Sickness and Road Trips

I have told y'all I have two kiddos who cannot throw up in the toilet to save their lives. Literally. It looks like an exorcism if they ever get a stomach bug. But the other side of that parenting nightmare is my two kids who can make it in the toilet nice and neat, are my two kids who get horribly car sick. Like car sick the moment the minivan would leave the driveway when they were little. Car sick on the way to the grocery store around the corner. Car sick just by the thought of driving. It was a horrible way to live my life when they were little and would just randomly vomit in my car. Just randomly vomit. No warning. Just threw up all over the whole damn backseat.

Oh sure, we had plans of it all landing in gallon size Ziplock bags. We bought peppermints and real cokes to take on trips to help instantly settle a stomach. Medicines. Holistic healing aids. Tips and tricks from any website on the internet. Spare clothes galore. Wet wipes. Windows rolled down. Airing out a car on the side of the road. We tried screaming and yelling a bunch, but that never ever worked. I tried losing my shit on a regular basis while crying and driving down the highway with my backseat and two children covered in vomit. That proved useless too. Car sickness. It's just a real bad situation.

We have 9 million children (or really just four), but we cannot afford airfare for six people ever so, road trips it is. And when they were little it was a sandwich of fun memories and mom losing her mind hosing down children and a minivan covered in puke. I'm sure these moments will live in infamy long after I'm gone. They stand frozen in time as some of my worst parenting moments ever. I have no apologies. It catches you off guard every single time. Vomit sucks.

We were driving to Arlington once from Katy, Texas. And traffic getting out of Houston is godawful. It's like nothing you have ever experienced, but it is a necessary experience if you ever want to find out what you are truly made of...It should be a requirement for all engaged couples. Can you stand the test of stop and go traffic and merging and lane closures and construction on I-35 together with four kids in a minivan. It can break you in a minute flat. But add in a side of car sickness and you will find out whether or not you are ready for life as a parent. This can be a deal breaker on the road to building a family.

We had been on the highway for no more than half an hour. We had hit one of those pockets where you were suddenly going 80 mph again, and you took full advantage. But moments prior we had been stop and go. Stop and go. Grace was greenish grey. She had her head resting on the side of her seat. Not speaking. Looking like a cross between The Walking Dead and a precious little girl doing her best to hold it together. There is a look only a parent can see right before the vomit spews. And I saw it. Instantly I was frantically pressing the button for her window and screaming at her (no calming tones or sweet cadences) to stick her head out the window.

We had Grace and Josh in the minivan captain chairs. Josh a hostage in his car seat. While Jude and Jake took up the back seat. All spread out. Ready for four hours of road trip hell. Made worse only by the fact that their little sister was instantly car sick, and there were hours upon hours to go.

Her head was out the window with waves of vomit coming one after the other. The passengers of vehicles passing us were gagging and staring…trying to look away…but their eyes were drawn to the beautiful blonde-haired angel with the fountain of rancid highway puke streaming out of our car. We were used to this experience by now. And never slowed the minivan. It would be over as soon as it started. No need to pull over. Just get it out the window as quickly as possible and keep on trucking.

"Jesus! No!" We heard it from the backseat.

"Oh God! Mom! No!" And it felt like slow motion. I turned in my seat.

Jake was covered. Covered. In the backseat. His face. His shirt. His whole non-vomiting person. Covered in Grace's puke.

Corey was like a man on a mission. Get your head back in the car. Drive through traffic and vomit. Don't stop. Don't abort the mission. Just hand out half assed apologies when necessary, and drive.

"Jake. There's nothing we can do." He shouted from the driver's seat. "Take your shirt off. Wipe your face off. We are not stopping for anything."

Parents everywhere who have driven through diapers and lost sippy cups and portable DVD players that quit working and car ride fights that rival World War Three totally get this…Don't stop…Throw a tourniquet on the problem…Just keep driving…

Jake drove shirtless that day. And we couldn't stop laughing. He was "that guy" when we went through a drive through…That random guy shirtless in a minivan ordering a burger. That random shirtless guy when you looked at the car next to you…just hanging out shirtless in a minivan. That shirtless guy sitting in the car at a gas station in nowhere Texas…seemed to fit right in.

He was shirtless with no explanation to the other road trippers we met along the way. He was shirtless and in jeans which made it somehow even more hysterical. The shirtless teen in jeans helping get trash out of a minivan while his dad pumped gas. Try it sometime. Just be shirtless in jeans in a car with no explanation…You instantly become a little white trashy. It's one of the best parenting experiences I have ever had…Made all the vomit worth it.

And don't worry. We made it to my mom's house a million hours later. Jake a little chilly from going shirtless in a minivan that had to have windows rolled down about every 15 to 20 minutes. But I feel like it made a man of him. Which is all you really ever want to happen when dragging your kiddos for hours upon hours in a van filled with puke and your asshole family that randomly still laughs about your shirtless journey.

Underwear as Only Wear

I don't know what it is about my children…maybe you have the same experience…maybe you scoff at families like mine…But my children, till way too late in life, just walk around in underwear as their "only wear". They don't care who sees them…I mean, shit y'all, everyone has seen them, talked to them, spent way too much time with them…in nothing but their underwear. It's apparently the only item of clothing they ever need.

It started with Jake and Jude. Living life in their diapers and pull ups. And morphed into dinners and play dates and family or friend affairs where they immediately stripped down for comfort. It was shocking with the first kiddo, but as time as gone on, it doesn't even phase me a bit with Josh. Always a kid at the dinner table…no matter who's dinner table…with nothing but underwear. Currently, Josh has spent three solid days at my Dad's house in nothing but Hanes boxer briefs and an occasional pair of socks. We beg him to get dressed for outings. He halfway obliges us. He halfway does not understand, "No shirt No shoes No service". No pants too. They don't serve you pant less either, buddy.

Not long ago, Jake was coming home to surprise Jude and Grace, and Josh was the only one who knew. He had just learned how to tie his shoes (yes, a little late in life at 9 years old, but I can't care too much about that either), and it was such a big accomplishment to him. He wanted to show Jake his newly tied-by-himself laces so, in order to get ready for him to walk through the door, Josh wore undies and his tennis shoes. Outfit complete for a surprise homecoming. Always a fashion statement by far. This is just how we live now.

We used to have a countdown with Jake and Jude when we went to people's houses. How long will we wait before they walk back out in their underwear? It's so weird because this would NEVER fly in the adult world. Hey, let's hang out sometime. And no matter if it is the first time or the 88th time you hang out, within five minutes get into your underwear. Don't ask either. Just assume it's a welcome practice for new friends.

Really, I am just placing this little piece of info in this lovely book so you know you're not alone…whoever you are…Stop pleading for clothing and just roll with it. I mean, if we all could feel this level of security and comfort the world would at least be a more interesting place. Just getting comfy at work and wearing your undies while you talk to clients…Maybe Covid brought us this little wave of peace and let down your hairness…

We will be begging the 9-year-old to throw on a pair of pants for Thanksgiving and Christmas this year. We will know that all of our cousins will be shockingly aware that Josh likes the striped Hanes boxer brief the best. And no need to worry about weather or temperature either…Undies are for all climates…Just wear them always…no pants needed at The Hooks House. All are welcome here. Pantless? Just join us. You'll fit right in.

The Universal Sign for Choking

Several years ago, I was at a party. Lots of people. Lots of kids. It may have been a barbecue. It may have been a potluck. There were people I knew well. And people I did not know at all. Packed house. And good, yummy food. I felt great. Except for this horrible sore throat. And I mean horrible. Like could barely swallow horrible.

It was so bad I had gone to the doctor the day before. And I rarely go see a doctor. And the doctor had looked at my throat, done some cultures and diagnosed me. With a sore throat. It was red. It hurt like hellfire. And that was it. Nothing. Nothing else. Just a really sore throat. I think he told me to take Tylenol.

So, we went to this party and every once in a while, I swallowed down delicious food while wincing in pain. I didn't want to draw attention to myself. But it hurt so bad. People noticed. They noticed how painstakingly I chewed my food…and I was barely eating…sure sign that something is wrong with Jackie Hooks. This girl loves food, and a buffet is like heaven to me. But the damn sore throat was ruining my life.

My friend, Tana, who was the greatest hostess, took pity on me. She listened to all my symptoms…which was only one…an extremely sore throat. And she had the sure-fire cure. Promised she used it on all her family. Swore it would save the day. And handed me a tiny bottle of Oregano Oil. Just a tiny little bottle. Told me to put three drops in a small amount of water. Gargle it. DON'T DRINK IT. It will burn a little. It will definitely burn a little. But you will be healed. And free to eat and drink and be merry. This sounded too good to be true. But I was willing to try anything because I was at a party with food, and I couldn't eat which is a chubby girl's nightmare.

Before I launch into this story, there is one thing you should know. I am a mother. I am a teacher. I have been trained. I have been trained in the Heimlich Maneuver. I have been trained in how to exit a car in a flash flood. I have been trained in CPR. Fire safety. Hurricane evacuation. Tornado sheltering. Nosebleeds. Simple First Aid. How to tell if a child has the flu or just the common cold. Stomach bugs and crackers. Minor arguments and major arguments between toddlers. How to avoid folding fitted sheets. The quickest way to make Mac-N-Cheese. Getting gum out of hair. How many towels make a washing machine shake and break. What all you can make popsicles out of (not beer). Is it a fart or is it a shart. And about 982 random trainings. Oh. And the Universal Sign for Choking. I got that one in the bag. Mainly I just wonder if I will ever have to use these life lessons. But I'm ready. Always ready. I'm a woman. These lessons are all filed away in my brain and waiting for the perfect moment.

So, here I stood at the kitchen sink, Oregano oil in hand. Now, I need to explain to y'all what the kitchen format was like. The sink faced the living room and dining room. It was an open concept. There was a long bar the sink was actually in, and the food for the party was lined all down this bar. Party goers would come up to the bar to get their food. And drinks. And from where I stood waiting to be healed by Oregano, I could reach out and touch anyone in the buffet line. We were less than a foot apart. But, even with the warning "it will burn a little", I was not worried one bit about the proximity with unsuspecting party goers. I wasn't worried about what these folks may witness. I wasn't worried about the throat burn…surely, I could handle it…I had been living with a throat on fire. So, a little burn to get to the healing would be worth it. No pain, no gain. We know the saying. I was going to live it…but just a little.

I put three drops of the oil into what amounted to a shot of water. I stood over the sink. The smell of Oregano was strong. Even with the tiny amount. And I was poised. Ready to knock it back like a girl reliving her college days. I counted down in my head. 3-2-1…And began to gargle…getting the mixture as far back in my throat as I could…without drinking it…I could instantly feel the burn…it was going to work. I just knew it. The pain would come with throat saving gain.

The burn started like a good type of pain. The kind that says there is a healthy throat on the other side. And then within about 2.2 seconds my throat was ablaze. I don't mean it hurt. I mean it hurt so bad I couldn't think straight. The burn was nuclear. And I was standing in front of a buffet line of people. Trying all of a sudden to die inconspicuously. Just die with my throat on fire at a sink at a party. This was my fate now, but damn, it was going to be an embarrassing death. I couldn't die in front of them. They would be traumatized for sure. And some weird vanity kicked in where I was just mortified of my impending death by Oregano oil.

It didn't take long for me to realize I could not breathe at all. The oil. The pain. The super sore throat. It combined. I was sweating from my eyebrows. This was new. And sweat poured out of the upper area of my cheeks which had honestly never happened to me or anyone I knew ever before. Eyebrow and upper cheek sweat must be synonymous with death by throat fire. And I was the only girl in the world who knew. Because I could tell no one. And they were all happy. My death would ruin the party. And I couldn't ruin a party.

I walked quickly, silently dying in agony, away. Just walked away. I would die alone; I decided on the guest bathroom. Someone would find me someday. It would be like the 1800's where women were in the kitchen and then just died of things like sore throats. I get that now. You just died where you were because the sore throat was clearly deadly. And I stood with my deadness in the bathroom. Sweating from weird new pores. And wondering if the intense lava in my throat would eventually melt my esophagus.

I took a moment to realize I could not even cry for help. I thought about how weird it was to sweat profusely from my eyebrows. And took into account the warning of the burning was definitely not sufficient. She should have said that I could have chosen Oregano Oil or a blow torch. The outcome was the same. And then I did the oddest thing I have ever done. In a moment of near death, I stood, staring at my reflection in the bathroom mirror, and did the universal sign for choking to myself. I was ready. I had been waiting to use this signal. And the time was NOW. I used that universal signal for all it was worth.

I stood. Both hands clasped around my neck signaling to myself that I could not breathe. In utter silence I signaled. To no onlookers. Zero rescue team. Not an EMT in sight in that guest bathroom. Just me. In silence. Telling me. I was in need of help. And oxygen. I pleaded with my eyes to the girl whose face was a mess of sweat. The drama was real. The hope was gone. But I knew the signal, and

I would make sure the universal sign for choking was used…and used well.

This is what some good solid training at some point in your life will get you…The ability to use a signal…I mean, I used the fuck out of that signal…Unfortunately, it was to no one. I was a goner. But I was a goner with the knowledge that the girl in the mirror was prepared to use a universal sign even if no one saw her. I was like the bear shitting in the woods…or the tree falling in the woods…whatever that saying is…I was it. And I didn't make a sound. Just a sign.

I look back on this moment and think of my sheer desperation. I look back and think how clearly I held that signal like it mattered. All the years of wondering if I would ever need to use the universal sign for choking…and I finally found the moment…just didn't find the people to share it with…And couldn't seem to rationalize walking out of the guest bathroom to save my life.

And just like that it passed. Breath back in my lungs. And my throat felt amazing. I mean, amazing. No sign of the moment I had just lived through. And I put my hands down. Wiped my odd sweat from my face, and just went back to the damn party. I was embarrassed to be myself with myself…if that makes since. I was embarrassed to know what I had just done in the bathroom even though the only person in the bathroom was me. Humbled by me. And I left that bathroom and the one woman rescue behind. And walked back in the kitchen like there wasn't just the most melodramatic ending to a made for TV movie ever. Just back to my normal life in the 21st century full of normal non 1800's death sentences.

And ate some appetizers. Like a good chubby girl does after she almost dies in the guest bathroom.

This near-death experience brought the use of Oregano Oil into my home. We use it for everything now. Every sniffle. Every faint mention of throat irritation. Every time a kid says they feel even the slightest under the weather. The people in my home are handed Oregano Oil and told to take it back like they are at a house party. They hate it. But it so fucking works. Now we know that folks everywhere and of all ages can experience eyebrow sweat and upper cheek sweat too. But this is now the only training that will actually save us. Oregano Oil. Order some. Catch your throat on fire for a minute. Just don't do it in the middle of a party. Poor choices. I will make them for you so you can learn from my "What NOT to do at a Party" survival guide.

A Little Thanksgiving Tumble

We had made the drive to Nashville. It was Thanksgiving time, and for us and our Nashville family that means we celebrate Thanksgiving and Christmas and birthdays all in one week. I drove up early with the kids the moment they were out of school, and Corey would join us later in the week...flying in on some Tuesday or Wednesday when he could get away from work. The kids and I had lived through the usual vomit fest with car rides and car sickness. We had stopped a million times because people were still halfway potty training and bladders were little. These were the days before Joshua. When my oldest was still super young and I had to hold hands everywhere we went. We have a road trip course laid based on Starbucks, Chick Fil As and Targets...The three tried and true places with the cleanest bathrooms. It matters when you have little kids.

But, nonetheless, we made it. And Corey had finally arrived too. The holidays could officially begin.

My dad has a pretty steep staircase in his house leading down to another bedroom and bathroom and a laundry room too. During these chaotic, little kid-filled visits he would block off the staircase by any means necessary. Old doors, rope, boards of any kind, ensuring little feet would not touch the stairs unassisted. Making sure it was safe. The way you do when a whole gaggle of children come wildly into your home. Temporary safety measures at every turn. Pretty much adults only navigated those stairs because we could handle the steepness. Let me rephrase that...In THEORY we could handle the steepness.

I don't even really know how it happened, although I watched the entire thing unfold. Corey was headed down the stairs...Had stepped over all the blockades and was walking downstairs. Like a normal person. Not too fast. Not distracted. And he just lost his footing. Just lost all his footing. Out of thin air it appeared his footing just failed him, and a slow-motion tumble would ensue right before my eyes.

I was on the stairs behind him and watched in horror as his feet came out from under him. He grabbed for the railing with both hands. He seemed to twist as he was going down. Shouting and grappling for anything to stop the impending fall. A guttural noise arose from inside him. And I was shocked as it happened...His foot went through a light in the wall. Just went through the whole fucking light in the wall. Stuck straight in and apparently very painful. He was yelling and cussing up a storm. With his foot inside the staircase wall.

At this point everyone gathered around the stairs. Corey still stuck by his foot in the wall. "What the hell happened?" Was the question of the moment. And Corey wasn't real sure. I think this is the point where we headed solidly into middle age. When you can't name the cause of a tumble down a staircase, welp, you might not be as young as you used to be.

"Are you ok?" Was clearly the next question on the menu. And the answer was just as uncertain. Corey removed his foot from the wall, and it was very apparent his baby toe had taken the brunt of that fall. Cut. Bleeding. Damaged. In need of some pretty immediate repair. We decided to head to an ER since it was Thanksgiving and nothing was open. All we needed was a stitch or two for the tiniest toe of all.

The ER was not packed. It had a few Thanksgiving veterans who had lost a battle with a knife or an oven or maybe even a turkey frier…Nothing major…And we fit right in with our far less than agile story of a staircase and some lost footing. Having to answer a few times over the course of our stay that my husband was not yet drunk at 10am.

We filled out the mountain of paperwork and sat in vinyl chairs with a toe wrapped in enough gauze to treat a significant head wound. We talked at great length about patience. And I tried to recount the tale with worry in my voice as opposed to the laughter that kept trickling out…I mean, y'all, his foot was stuck in the wall. It was priceless. It didn't take all too long for us to get seen. And the male nurse had a shockingly high-pitched voice. Shockingly high pitched. Which is horrible for two assholes who can never make eye contact in serious situations. It sounded like Mickey Mouse was our nurse for the day, and I had to excuse myself about 982 times due to the fact that I kept laughing.

Over and over Mickey Mouse was talking about tiny toes, and I was in over my head trying to keep a straight face. Corey was in it thick with me. He was just laughing. We looked like two stoners living through a Thanksgiving adventure gone wrong…Laughing hysterically at nothing with a near severed toe and a story of staircase missteps which barely made any since at this point.

Mickey Mouse left and came back with a doctor, and they approached Corey with the news: No stitches today…They had landed on a possible amputation. For the love of fuck. Are you kidding me? They had decided to cut off his baby toe.

And my husband lost it. He was laughing and saying, "You're going to amputate my toe?" He reminded them he had been a medic, a surgical tech and had worked in medicine his whole life. "You're not going to cut off my fucking baby toe." And I knew they hated us. I would have hated the laughing couple who were clearly off their rocker with a toe hanging in the balance.

The nurse and doctor walked away, and my husband looked at his wife who was holding her stomach from the pain of constant laughter. "They are not gonna take my toe." And I knew he meant it.

We gathered our things. Looked both ways. Looked around corners. And ran. We ran like his toe depended on it. Corey was hobbling in an almost sprint and I was close behind with my purse and our jackets feeling like America's Most Wanted. Thinking only of a tiny toe still deserving of a chance on this planet.

We sped out of the parking lot like we had just won it all at a casino…like Thelma and Louise…like we had just robbed a bank and lived to tell the tale…The toe would make it to see another day…We were the champions…

That Thanksgiving we took lots of care of a little toe. Wrapping and re-wrapping with gauze and band aids cut down to itty bitty toe size. I think Corey still has some feeling loss years upon years later, but all in all the toe is functioning as a baby toe should.

And the hole is still somewhat in the wall. The staircase lighting he took out that day still bears the scar of a rogue foot making a surprise attack. And the truth of the matter became clear, the older you are the harder the stairs. We hate it when we settle on a new truth, but young people navigate stairs with easy breezy carefree lives…It's us older folks in need of rails and padding and maybe a solid guide…

And don't forget, marry someone who will escape from an amputation with you…no matter how seemingly insignificant an amputation…Marry the person who throws medical advice to the wind and makes a break for it…Those are your people…Never a dull moment when you're running to save the life of a baby toe.

Black Friday…Kinda

I have only been Black Friday shopping once. And it was only kinda. I was really just a tag along with my husband, but I wanted to feel the intensity and the fever of scoring a deal. I am almost certain in this story he was looking for a TV. Almost certain. It's like his constant quest in life every few years so, I am going to just assume it was a TV we were out and about trying to get a hot deal on…

But wait. I don't want you thinking we were out at midnight or 3am. Think more along the lines of 3:00PM. More along the lines of making a few calls to some local Walmarts to see if the TV and the deal were still available. The rush was over. The long lines did not exist. This was a Black Friday adventure completely for the faint of heart. For the folks who just wanted a new TV at a good price…Zero intensity whatsoever. But let me remind you, I WANTED the intensity…not the early hours…but the intensity sounded really cool.

And I had eyed a great deal on a little Disney Princess satin comforter and sheet set. Grace had a toddler bed at this time and she was in love with every Disney Princess. And I thought, "Hey! I can ride shotgun on this adventure and purchase a little Christmas present for my girl at half the price."

Don't worry. There were loads of these comforter sets still available. This clearly was not what most Black Friday shoppers had fought over in the early hours of the morning. There was no scuffle for the satin junior bed comforter set. And I walked back to the area where a mound of them was still displayed and easily grabbed one from Santa to Grace. No pushing. No yelling. No elbows thrown. The store was working at a normal pace. People milling around. Just a lazy Friday afternoon feel of a typical Walmart.

My phone dinged alerting me to a text message from Corey, "You've gotta hurry." Was all I needed.

I knew it. There was a second wave. There was probably a crowd beginning to swell. And my heart started pounding. This was it. This was late afternoon Black Friday. And I was starting to sweat. I had to get this satin comforter set out of here…I had to make a run for it.

I ran. I ran faster than my legs could logistically carry me. The aisles were empty, but I kept running. Scouring every turn for signs of my husband. I got lost twice. And ran even faster. I was at the front of the store, and I started just shouting his name, "Corey! Corey!" Blinded by the notion that I had to hurry…Black Friday was upon me.

I caught a glimpse of him. He was already at the cash register. No lines. No swarms of angry shoppers. No yelling or pushing. But my heart was beating louder than logic in my ears, and I just kept running.

I pushed past an elderly couple looking for gum, and threw the comforter set onto the conveyor. Threw it. Y'all. Onto the conveyor. My husband in this moment looked so confused. And my feet slipped out from under me. I landed in the empty aisle beside the couple who now had a pack of gum in their hands, with a thud. Face first. But I had made it.

"What the hell are you doing?" Corey asked like a husband who wished I was his distant cousin at this point.

"You told me to hurry. It's Black Friday." I said from the floor.

"Jackie. I was just about to check out. You didn't have to hurry like THAT."

We paid. We walked silently to the car. In an empty parking lot. Nodding our goodbyes to the couple with gum.

But truth be told, the glory was in the running. I felt Black Friday in my soul. The glory was in the make-believe hurry and worry and deals for the taking. I felt it y'all. And I was never asked to go with my husband again.

Set it on Fire

Corey and I had been married for less than a week. We were honeymooning in New Orleans, and it was a party. I've already told y'all we were party people, and it's true. So, New Orleans took it to a whole new level for us. There was a point where Corey ended up in a parade. Lots of eating yummy food. Lots of bar hopping. Lots of fun. We were newlyweds and everywhere we went we were super side by side…ordering drinks with breakfast lunch and dinner.

Now, Corey was still in the Navy at this point. He had travelled around part of the globe and knew all the things about all the drinks. He made my college days look like child's play.

We walked into a bar early in the afternoon because there was a live band playing. Walked straight up to the bar, and Corey ordered a shot of 151. I have to be honest with you, I still don't know exactly what 151 is…But it's something he wanted, and he was certain.

The bartender put a shot on the bar and looked annoyed with us instantly. We were half drunk and young and being way too cute for his tastes. He was big and bald and beyond all the bullshit.

I felt like Corey wasn't catching the vibe this guy was throwing. He proceeded to launch into some story before taking his shot, and the guy behind the bar looked like he would rather stab himself in the shoulder than listen to us. Corey just kept on talking and ended by telling him to set his shot on fire.

"You don't want to do that, man." He said with the enthusiasm of a corpse.

And Corey launched into another story explaining how he and his Navy buddies always light their 151 on fire. And requested it be lit again. And when I say Corey was "explaining" things to this bartender who thought we were akin to Margo and Todd from "Christmas Vacation", I mean, Corey was really really overly explaining things to this man who hated us. But Corey insisted on the lighting of this shot of 151.

"Hey man, you don't want to do that." To which Corey became adamant.

"I think I know what I'm talking about, buddy." Oh shit. Did he just really call the bartender buddy?

"Hey Corey, I think he's really telling you not to do this." I tried.

But Corey was dug in and began explaining again how he ALWAYS lights his 151 on fire. Apparently, he had been drinking blazing shots ALL THE TIME. I mean, I had never actually seen any of this, but clearly, he loved shots on fire at this point in time and was going down with the ship if needed with flames coming from a shot of 151.

The bartender pulled out a lighter. Rolled his eyes. Looked like he was about ready to kick Corey's 151 drinking ass and lit the shot on fire.

Corey knocked it back instantly.

"I was trying to tell you the shot glass is plastic." The bartender said as Corey started to grab his mouth.

And I watched as my brand-new husband began to remove burnt plastic from his top lip which was already beginning to blister.

The bartender smiled and walked away.

And, you guessed it, I was left with laughter. I couldn't stop. His lips were so swollen. And it was such a lesson in don't be an asshole to the bartender…He just might have a tiny yet very important piece of information you desperately need to hear.

A Tray of Hot Coco

When I was in 9th grade, I was accompanying my older sister on a volleyball trip. Or we were picking her up from a volleyball camp. I can't actually remember at all which it was. But we were there, and she was there and it was in Austin, Texas circa 1988 maybe. I found myself as the only non-volleyball person at a very large restaurant table of Volleyball players and their parents.

I remember feeling a touch out of place. And in those days, you couldn't hide your awkwardness by playing on your phone, you had to sit there in silence or make random conversation. I was maybe 14 at this time, and so, like so many fantastic teens throughout time, I chose silence. It felt like I was invisible at the same time as it felt like everyone was talking about me which sums up adolescents pretty well. So, I sat at a table looking like I didn't care about anything in the world and hating everyone simultaneously. It's a great look. Don't worry, your teens will show it to you regularly.

The waiter finally came to the table, and if my memory serves me, it was some sort of breakfast place. Every single girl at the table ordered hot chocolate. Including me. And the waiter said that he would be back to take our orders in a minute. And probably went to the kitchen to spit in the 4 million hot cocos he was about to make for the asshole table of adolescent girls. So much Shimmering Shell lipstick and braces.

It took forever. And the girls on the team were all laughing and talking while I mastered the art of looking bored. I was super annoyed with my parents for even existing so, I was being extra rude to them too. Seriously. This age and stage in life is so fun. And the waiter was taking forever and ever. And I had done the teenage thing of not dressing for the weather. I was freezing in my Laura Ashley jumper which was meant for the summer clearly...and it was winter break. I needed that hot coco more than life itself. It was all that was keeping me from murdering everyone around me.

I could see the waiter coming back. He was clearly trying to be efficient. He had an enormous circle tray. And I thought, "Man. That is a dumb choice." It was filled with just about 982 hot cocos. Steam was pouring from every mug. And I watched him half amused to see how he would handle this situation. In the bitchy way of a grumpy teen, I smiled inside waiting to see his dismount of this incredibly overburdened tray. There was way too much hope in his eyes.

He wove his way between tables and chairs. And was walking toward our table. Slowly. I was sitting at the head of the table because I wanted to talk to no one but be noticed by everyone. I watched him work this out inside his head. You could tell his wheels were turning, and he was realizing he had not thought this through at all. He moved his hand ever so slightly as if to begin to set the tray on the table. Like he had just imagined himself effortlessly setting a piping hot tray of 2700 hot cocos down on a table of teen girls and their families with zero mishaps or obstacles. His eyes were way too determined. He was going in and setting this bitch on the table.

I watched his hand and arm not know what to do. I watched the tray teeter and totter and give way. The entire tray. It just gave way. And the whole thing landed on my head. Cup after cup of hot coco landed on my head. Pouring down my shoulders and the entirety of my perfectly sculpted hair. Mugs were crashing to the floor, and hot liquid was scalding my legs. The boiling water just kept coming. There were so many mugs. So many mugs. And whipped cream. It was everywhere.

"Are you ok????" Came from every direction. And I was so stunned. And my legs were on fire. And I was mortified. And my parents were trying not to laugh. And my sister was laughing HYSTERICALLY. And I went with the nonchalant teen thing of wearing the attitude of, "This may be annoying, but it is so no big deal to me…honest." As I died inside.

I rinsed off as much of everything as I could in the bathroom. Put my hair in the sink a little. It was the late '80's and no one cared about their children yet or their emotional wellbeing so, the whole table just ordered and ate as I cleaned up in the bathroom. No change of clothes was offered because we had to get on the road. God y'all. It was the 1980's so everyone piled in the car with a girl who was a sticky burnt mess and drove home for three and a half hours. Stuck the headphones of my Walkman through the sticky matted mess of my hair and stared into oblivion. It was a different time.

But it was these exact times that made me…the comedian watching other people's humiliating stories unfold as I laugh and laugh and laugh. My own stories too. Kids just had to get over themselves and move on with life with sticky hair or slight burns or horrible attitudes. Everyone just light your cigarettes and smoke in the car with the windows rolled up…We will all be fine.

I'm sure today we raise healthier children with better social and emotional well-being…But take a kid from the 1980's, 1970's, 1960's and leave them out in a wilderness with maybe a deck of cards, some RC Cola, jean shorts and a sweatshirt and we can make it just fine.

And it's somewhere in this mentality that my children are stuck with me. Somewhere along the way I just quit caring so much and started laughing way more. Somewhere along the way I just decided to love my horrible children the way they are and feel thankful that these foul-mouthed assholes are mine all mine. And I hope you feel the same about yours too.

But remember, when seated at a table of maybe 50, forego the hot coco…especially if your waiter looks like he's ready for the world. He is not. He is not ready for the world at all. And he has no plan. And the coco will inevitably go on your head if your last name is Hooks…I promise. Just order a fountain drink and pour it on your own damn head.

Really Opens Up My Bowels

Years ago, Corey was at one of those bougie men's haircut places. I can't remember why he decided he needed to spend the money, but he had heard it was amazing and decided to set some cash on fire for a haircut. He was super excited to go. Super excited to have the haircut of his life. And he kept telling me they massage your face and wrap it in a hot towel. Which totally sounded incredible and worth all the money. I mean, heck. I would pay good money to let someone rub my face too and put a hot towel on it while I sit there alone. Take my whole wallet. Who cares at that point. Sounds like a dream come true for real.

So, Corey got the haircut of a lifetime. Which looked pretty much the same as usual. But apparently worth a lot more. And he walked in the door barely able to tell me about it because he just kept cracking up. He was laughing so hard he couldn't speak. The story goes something like this:

He sat down in the chair feeling a little out of place. This was a salon for God's sake, and he has lived his life in a walk-up barber shop/haircut place of the month/menu on the board type of situation. He tried to make a little small talk with the gal cutting his hair. In his words, "She was super hot", and rubbing the living daylights out of his face. He was nervous. A certain fish out of water feeling washed over him. So, he just kept chatting even as she wrapped his whole head in a steamy warm towel.

It was divine. It was like a slice of heaven on his face. He was out of his league, and he knew it. He did what The Hooks do best, and just kept talking. The gal was not responding, but she was there rubbing his shoulders. And he couldn't think of what else to say. She was hot. She was young. There was a hot towel. He was so flustered.

"Ahhhhhh. This is nice. It really…"

And what he intended to tell this goddess on earth was how it opened up his sinuses. Which in and of itself is a little weird and gross. I mean, he was roughly 40 at this point, and by that age we do really care about our sinuses. I mean, it's something you talk about with friends when you have been alive for a few decades. And he was chattering away. Trying to relax. But the sentence was already tumbling out of his mouth. And he stated, while she rubbed his shoulders…

"Ahhhhhh. This is nice. It really opens up my bowels."

Oh my God. What in the ever-living hell? He realized instantly he had just told the hairdresser he was shitting himself, or at the very least farting a lot due to the relaxation of a warm towel and a shoulder rub. His bowels were opened. She could thank herself for that one…

And he couldn't stop laughing. He was laughing so hard it was one of those completely silent laugh attacks…Where no sound comes out and you can't breathe. So, his sentence just hung in the air like he meant it. No retraction. Just the statement of his bowels being wide open. And the silence to follow.

I wish I could have been inside her head as she had to decide whether or not to step away from the middle-aged man with the loose bowels. I wish I could have seen her face or heard her tell her friends about the conundrum of the man who surely pooped himself after a hot towel to the face. But all I know is that this story might just live in infamy in someone else's favorite comedy. And my husband is the star.

He went back to his regular hair cut place after that day. No need to forget who you are for a second. Corey Hooks is clearly not a bougie hot towel kind of guy. We can't keep it together to be invited back to the fancy places.

Swollen and Stuck

I don't often get pedicures. I mean, it is so infrequent that I can actually tell you I am probably with my mom in Arlington, TX if it ever happens. She goes all the time. Knows all the people working. Has special things just for her. She is loved and adored with her manicured hands and toes. Me. Not so much.

I remind myself to shave my legs before I go. I try to take off the remnants of toenail polish from who knows how long ago. Sometimes it's like 18 layers of nail polish caked on from a summer of making things work. I remember to wear stretchy pants. Work out pants are best. This is the number one thing I remind myself: Stretchy pants. The type you can wistfully pull up over your thick calves and fluffy knees. I know this because of the world's worst swelling incident ever to take place at a nail salon. It lives in history as one of the most stressful 15 to 20 minutes of my life.

I was home for something...staying with my mom, and as always, she took me for a pedicure. As is the norm, I typically see people I know from my time in Arlington...High School friends, old teachers, people from a church we once went to...you name it, people from my past. It makes me happy. I get to chat for a little bit and hear about their lives. Sometimes, however, it brings me anxiety to see people I used to know...For instance, if they are old family members who we had a falling out with and keep our distance from...They aren't "bad" people...just the people who you hope you actually look your best in front of due to a million pounds of insecurity.

On this particular day at the nail salon, no one was there…it was just a few of us and the place was small, so we chatted with strangers while folks took a cheese grater to my Hobbit feet. I had on jeans, and I had worked a little too hard to get them onto my knees…they wouldn't go over my knees…just onto them…stuck there, if you will, like the wedding band on my finger…I mean, I can probably get my wedding band off, but it's going to take some work and some sort of lubricant and I might not be able to get it back on…But alas, weight gain is what it is and it doesn't typically throw you into a shame spiral about your knees.

My jeans were up, my feet were hanging in the warm water and the chair massager was going full throttle. The feet hanging was most likely a problem…causing a bit of a swelling feeling…but nothing major…just my usual swollen ankles and feet…this is the wear and tear of queso and chips for 40 plus years. It's the price we pay.

I was so happy. And I wasn't even going to feel bad about my off-color toenails…picked an opaque polish and I was ready to feel better about flip flops in the future. Here I was with my mom and a little needed pampering until the door opened and a distant family member on my husband's side walked in the door. And I took a deep breath, sat up a little straighter, and thought about all the amazing things my four children were doing and a laundry list of accolades for my husband as well as pleasant anecdotes to remind her we were really good people worthy of praise.

It's such an odd feeling, but it happens…the brag and dash…it's anxiety ridden for me, but if the random person arises who might just tell my enemies how well I am doing, welp, I am ready with my less than honorable list of awards and Nobel Prizes given to my people.

We said our "Hellos", and I was reading through the list of the awesomeness of The Hooks Family. It was going well. We had moved past platitudes and were into some regular conversation and small talk. I felt on edge, but more at ease. I was ok. It was ok. This moment in time would pass pleasantly and I would go back to my mom's house and feel halfway decent again. We passed the time with a little laughter, and it was time to go. Water was drained from the foot basin, flimsy disposable flip flops were in place, my mom was paying at the register…I was left with a few more moments of small talk. I could do this. I'm good at light banter. The end was in sight.

I perched my feet on the side of the basin and began to pull at my jeans. I worked a little harder than usual to get them past my knees, but I didn't think much of it. And the next step was simple: pull my jeans from below my knees to my ankles…nothing fancy…one sweeping motion…And nothing happened. Nothing happened at all.

Apparently, my calves had swollen tight. Tight y'all. They looked like horrible balloons that could pop with a tiny poke of a pin. I kept talking while I pulled some more, and I began to sweat. Like red faced wine sweat…I was hot…I was flustered and the more I pulled the more no movement took place. How was this happening to me? How was I giving so much comedy ammunition away for free? And to the last person on earth, I wanted to walk away and say, "I saw Jackie today. Her calves are in need of liposuction and she's wearing capris permanently after today."

"Honey, are your pants stuck?" The older family member I was trying to impress asked me.

God, it stung. So many things I wanted to say. So much shame in the pointless tugging at my pant legs to get over my god forsaken calves. So much hotness in my face. I drank a sip of water and downed the cup of free box wine…This was hell. Just hell. I didn't answer. No answer was needed. I was living out the answer in front of her.

I pulled and pulled, and the family member of days gone by got in there and pulled too. I was half laughing and half wanting to die. There was this quiet shock of pain and relentless exertion of energy with zero results. It felt like my calves were swelling more by the second. I blamed it on having four children…I blamed it on my slow metabolism…I blamed it on being over 40…And I knew that with this rhetoric of blame there was a mountain of shame that I would not give up queso and not go on a weight loss regiment once this moment had passed…Just live through this and not have to amputate a calf was my only hope.

Sweat was pouring down my face. My hands were red and sore from the denim nightmare. Two other people had joined in the trauma and were pulling with such force I could literally feel my lower legs being severed from my body. The nail salon was silent with the exception of an occasional, "Oh my goodness." And a, "Holy Shit." Here and there. This was my life now. This is what I had become. A big girl in a nail salon with tight jeans and large calves and an impeccable set of toenails. I gave up.

I stood with my extraordinarily tight now decidedly capri jeans and took a long deep breath. I thought of my family.

I thought of how quick the universe could turn on one woman. I thought of just grabbing scissors and going home in my panties. And I pulled one last time with the force of the sturdy woman I am...The jeans gave way...and I stood there...no dignity left and no feeling in my hands, calves or ankles. This is what is left of me...

And I hobbled out of the store trying to act like this was the most natural event of my lifetime. Waving goodbye. Gingerly wiping the sweat from my face using the lifeless meat hooks that had once been useful hands. It was over. And I left my pride somewhere on the salon floor along with a promise to only wear stretchy pants from here on out.

Y'all. Stretchy. Like Lycra times 10,000. Don't risk it. I'm here to help you heed this warning of a relaxing day turned into a wretched affair. Your calves are too important to needlessly amputate at a nail salon, and no one has time for the shame spiral caused by tight pants and above knee cuffs. This is my public service announcement to all my pear-shaped counter parts...Stretchy stretchy pants when getting pedicures. Save the tight jeans for standing room only. Trust me.

One Hot Crotch

I am not a frequent yoga girl. I have done it many times. I own a mat. I own some yoga friendly pants. But it's not something I do on the regular. I go on occasion when I'm invited by really just two friends…Tana or Claire. I typically try to make sure it is an easy class. Or a "flow" class. Or maybe just someone playing bowls and I get to lay there on my mat. I'm not in this for exercise. I'm in this for my friends and a little relaxation. Nothing more. Love it when I do it. Don't think about it until Claire or Tana invite me.

So, a couple of years ago Claire, who I affectionately named, Claire Bear, invited me and some others to do Hot Yoga with her. This actually sounded horrible to me. I mean, I love Claire Bear. I love warm weather. I love yoga pants. But I did not like the sound of being in a hot room and stretching with others nearby. Being in a hot room sucks. Honestly. I know. My classroom fluctuates some days between 49 and 982 degrees. But I was game for Hot Yoga for some reason…maybe checking off some yoga bucket list…maybe boredom…maybe sheer love of the epic Claire Bear…so, I said yes. Deciding to leave my expectations at the door and enjoy some hippy happy hotness.

I had recently bought some wonderful celadon green stretchy athletic pants…with a matching sports bra. Think the color of lettuce. So so so pretty. Lovely, unusual color. And I felt all sorts of earthy coolness putting them on. And driving with my barely used yoga mat to the yoga studio. All would be well. I would be the beginner in the class certainly, but hippy happy yoga people are super ok with beginners, and I would sit by Claire and feel confident she would keep me sane.

I arrived and loved the typical smell of incense and the vibe of the calming music. Everyone saying quiet hellos. Putting their mats down. Stretching. Drinking water. Feeling good and healthy. A bit overweight, but I have long hair so that makes up for it. And I may have noticed at this point everyone in their black yoga pants. Everyone. I may have noticed there was no color anywhere close to my lovely pale green pants. So tight. So stretchy. But no. Everyone was in their black yoga pants. Everyone.

The room was hot. Like can't breathe hot. Have a panic attack because you're baking hot. Feeling like you're in a coffin hot. But, nonetheless, I sat on my mat making super quiet polite conversation. Dry heat everywhere. And Claire and her group of yogis in black pants. Like it was a requirement of some sort, ready to bend in ways I only dreamed of in my youth.

Can I remind you I am not a small woman? Can I remind you my legs are not muscular? Can I remind you I am shaped exactly like a pear? A pear. Specifically, a celadon green shade of pear in my tight yoga pants. Ready. And hot. Like 100 degrees hot. Like too hot. And why were all these people in black pants? This was stupid. Black absorbs heat. Celadon green leafy lettuce cutie pie pants are much more heat resistant. How could I be smarter than everyone in the room with their goth black yoga pants?

It didn't take long into the stretching and breathing to realize a few things. First, it was damn hot. Second, black yoga pants camouflage your hot, steamy, very sweaty crotch. Black yoga pants hide the enormous circle of wet shame surrounding your inner thighs and crotch area. Black yoga pants disguise the fact that you look like you pissed yourself from the get-go and have even less care about the fact that the circle of sweaty shame will grow by the minute. But only at your crotch as if to mock you and remind the room you have one very hot crotch.

I remember doing a bendy move where I was staring at my hot crotch in its humbling circle of sweat, and wondering if there was some sort of yoga chat room where people were telling others that black only was the way to go with hot yoga…I mean, I had missed some crucial intel and here I was with the circle of death on the front of my vagina. I wanted so badly to quit sweating, specifically in my crotch, for at least a minute or two or three…

I didn't quit sweating. Don't worry. And I got a few, "Bless your heart…" stares from the skinny people in the room. Silly middle-aged pear-shaped girl feeling cute in your pants…Black exists for a reason in yoga communities. There is stuff to hide. Especially stuff making your crotch look like a hot mess.

I made it through the class. I got to the other side of the hot yoga universe and felt equally as refreshed as wishing I had a skirt to wear out of the room. As I walked toward the door feeling like an Amazon next to the men in the room who clearly wore XS tees, I wished someone would hand me a beach towel or possibly I could wrap my mat around my waist…Any option to not have to walk into the parking lot where others who had not just finished this class with me were parking…But, alas, there was no freedom from the knowledge of what not to wear.

When I stepped into my house where my judgmental asshole family lives, I knew I was walking into heckling from the crowd.

"Man. You got one hot crotch." Was all my husband said.

And I went to peel off the prettiest pants with the darkest shade of green crotch I had ever worn.

Shirtless Dad

Corey and I had just had our first baby. We were so young. We were so ill equipped. My goodness the thought of going out seemed overwhelming. And we only had one kid y'all. I can promise you by the time we had our fourth we were not nearly as crazy, and anxiety ridden as we were back in 2003 when Jake made his arrival. But in 2003 everything felt like a gamble. We felt like we were doing everything wrong, and we were like two months in...and carting out a baby in one of the heaviest baby carriers ever was beyond me...the diaper bag too...the mountains of supplies...I generally sucked at all of this...But a baby crying endlessly in public and not being able to be soothed felt like a death sentence. It was enough to make a hermit out of me...But we ventured out one cold winter night for a quick dinner with my parents. I can assure you this goes down in history as one of the very best nights of my life.

La Isla was a Mexican restaurant near our first house. Delicious queso. Chips. Salsa. Quesadillas. Everything I am in love with about food. And my parents were paying. And they would be there to help with the baby if things went awry. La Isla had these weird tiny walls to separate "rooms". The walls came up to maybe just above your hips. You could see everyone in the entire place if you stood. And everyone could see you easily the second you got to your feet. It was an odd set up to say the least, but not one you paid much attention to unless you stood. But we were sitting while eating so who even cares, right?

We were seated at a nice little table. And I instantly felt stressed trying to figure out how to get the baby carrier into this sling like thing to hold it...I don't even know if these exist anymore, but in 2003 they were at every restaurant. We could push Jake up to the table and he would balance precariously in this sling thing while still strapped in his 500-pound baby carrier. We could watch him sleep. Because when we arrived, he was sound asleep. And my hope and prayer and wish to the entire Universe was for him to sleep through the entire meal. He was bundled and swaddled and cuddled so tight. I think we even had a neck pillow around his head to keep him safe. And if he would sleep, welp, I could eat. That was my only thought as we sat down and grabbed menus. If he would sleep, I could eat.

The restaurant was loud with a mariachi band playing that night. My parents were so excited to be with their first grandchild. And we were happy. I was shoveling queso into my mouth in no time. And ordering a second bowl because I think I had barely had time to eat in the last few weeks with a newborn at home. Those times were so weird. No sleep. No shower. No regular food schedule. And here I was happily eating without shame in a lively restaurant with my little family. What could be better?

And then it began. The crying. And crying. And crying. Jake was like a tiny banshee. And I was beginning to freak out.

Jake was screaming in his baby carrier, and I was struggling to get him out. I couldn't figure out the straps fast enough and the sling was oddly balanced and the stares of other people who clearly were way better parents than me were hot on my shoulders. The waitress came by and offered to help, and that only made it worse. I hated her instantly. The young Mom Guilt and shame was filling my heart with panic.

My mom was giving suggestions and so was Corey...my stepdad sat watching as his family began to slowly unravel...I gave dirty looks to everyone just to make the dinner vibe real peaceful.

I got the baby out of the carrier and tried to give him a bottle. He wasn't having any of it. The crying got louder. I tried taking off some of his 9 million clothes because maybe he was hot. Not even a pause in his shrieking. And I was 27 years old with about zero tricks up my sleeve in a public place with tiny walls. I passed the baby off to my mom, and she gave it her best shot while telling me it was no big deal and babies cry...But whether it was true or not, I was certain the entire place was about to call CPS before we could order dinner.

Corey and I launched into one of the number one hits of parenting and marriage: If the moment is stressful, go ahead and start arguing. Just go for it. Blame each other. Or get real good and passive aggressive. It's a real treat for anyone within earshot and adds a lively kick to any meal. Trust me. And those tiny walls were allowing for a show stopping performance.

We continued whisper yelling while the baby screamed, and we passed him around the table. I was sweating. I knew people were staring. Corey said we should leave. And I stood to do the mom rock back and forth thing to get this baby back to sleep. It wasn't working, and I was certain the room was now 982 degrees. I think at this point I yelled at my mom too. Why not? She could deal with some unfounded anger from her daughter...I mean, she had raised me through the teenage years...it seemed appropriate to just blame her too.

Corey was dripping with sweat. He had on boots, jeans, a belt, a t-shirt with a fleece pullover over the top. Let me pause here to say that the fleece days of the late '90s and early 2000's did no one any favors while indoors. The stress of the baby who was still howling at the top of his lungs was too much. The whisper yelling with his wife who looked like a deranged lunatic with a screaming baby in her arms while still somehow managing to dip chips in queso was proving too much. The sweat was visible. He looked like he might have a heat stroke.

And he stood. He stood over those tiny waist high walls for the whole damn restaurant to see, ask the waitress to maybe turn on a fan in the middle of winter, announced to all around that he was hot and began the motion to take off his pullover to end his personal stress filled heatwave.

The movement was so quick. He did one of those pull over the back motions to get the fleece hot box off his back. And I was shocked. Mere seconds later my husband stood, the entire restaurant patronage watching aghast as they witnessed a man take his entire shirt off. His entire up top clothing. It all came off…pullover and t-shirt underneath…my shirtless husband still wearing jeans, a belt and boots…hairy white chest and belly on a one-man solo parade.

The mariachi band stopped.

All heads turned.

"What is he doing? Please make him stop." My mom asked and begged in a quiet whisper filled with shock and rage. The question was clearly the one everyone needed the answer to at this point. What is he doing?

And he just kind of stood there. Just stood still. He was just as shocked as us. The waist high walls seemed only to accentuate the shocking shirtlessness. And the belt. Well, the belt made it seem oddly dressed up for a no shirt kind of evening out.

The silence was everything.

I couldn't breathe, I was laughing so hard. I watched that man of mine wrestle his t-shirt out of his pullover and put it back on with the air of a stripper when the lights come on…"Oh Shit" simply hung in the room from every direction. No one could make eye contact with him. He was for sure the topic of conversation at every table watching him over teeny tiny walls. The man without a shirt just standing there. They probably still reference it today. What not to do in a crowded restaurant…We were the entire example that night.

We finished our meal. I mean, y'all, what more could we do. The baby quit screaming as babies eventually do…The mariachi band never made it to our table because every time they headed our way one of them would start to laugh so avoidance was probably best. But all in all, I learned a lot that winters night…

1) Wear a belt as often as possible. Really dresses up any casual attire.
2) Floor to ceiling walls are much more concealing.
3) Pull your overshirt off by the sleeves…you'll have better luck if you're planning on keeping your shirt on…But only if that's the plan.

4) Taking your shirt off while standing in a crowded restaurant really brings you and your in-laws together in a way you can't imagine. Truly. Try it. Bonded for life.
5) Finally, please Jesus, marry someone who will whisper fight with you while rocking a baby and eating queso…these types of people are fire…and that is what it's all about.

Grace's White Trash Dresser

Grace had asked for her 16th birthday present to have her room re-done. She had a list of things and pieces of furniture she needed moved and rearranged. Desks would change places. Her make up table would go in her closet. Removing artwork. Adding pieces. Creating a record listening area. A new floor to ceiling tapestry. A new bed with new bedding too. It was excellent, and a super fun birthday present to put into action. We set aside an entire Saturday to help make this idea into a reality. She was excited. We were excited. What could go wrong?

Well actually a lot can go wrong when rearranging a teenage room. There was spray paint involved. There were tape measures and things not fitting. The need for a shoe shelf became extremely apparent. And don't worry. We fought like 88 times that day. We had pulled old furniture out of the shed. We had repurposed more items than imaginable. And thrown clothes in all directions.

By the end of the day, we had arranged and rearranged the bedroom 982 times. Artwork had been placed in stacks of "want" and "don't want". And they were big, big stacks. The dogs were underfoot at every turn. And our joy had turned to desperation. We were desperate to be finished. We were desperate for Grace to be in love with the new room. We were desperate to get the last pieces of furniture moved, and we were worn out. We were all just plain worn out. Every hand was on deck. Even the 10-year-old was part of the labor.

And finally…finally…we were down to her hulking black dresser. It just had to be moved into the closet. No big deal. We had taken down closet rods and made a huge space for it. Just had to get it through the bathroom door and the closet door. It would be easy. It had to be easy. We had barely any strength left for this…But it was Grace's birthday wish. And she had drawn floor plans and made lists. We could do this. We are The Hooks dammit. We can do anything we set our minds to…

We pulled the drawers out. We turned it on its side. We shimmied it. We slid it. And it wasn't going without a fight. We were all yelling at each other. Dad was mad at everyone. None of us could figure out how to use our arms or hands or where to put our feet for that matter.

It was a dresser doorway nightmare of epic proportions.

As we scooched and scooted and cussed and sweated, Corey gave way to every emotion. He kicked the bottom of the dresser, and his foot went through. Dammit. But we were holding on. This dresser could not and would not beat us. Hole in the bottom be damned. Grace was going to use this dresser no matter its flaws.

We were now in the closet. The tightest squeeze with three dogs, four kids, my husband and me…This dresser was now where we would likely just live the rest of our lives. Just us. In a closet with a broken dresser. It would be our life story of the folks who lived their days in a closet because they couldn't figure out any passage to the rest of the house. Until this crazy monstrosity was in place, we could not vacate the closet. Simple as that.

We took a deep breath and pretty much all just cussed each other out. We flipped that dresser over to get it to its upright position. And a leg gave way. And I watched my husband muster all the strength he had left in him. He was a man who had been moving furniture all day. Over and over to new positions. Arrange and rearrange. Hanging pictures and painting furniture. He was a dad on the edge, and he was determined to get his trapped family out of this damn closet one way or another.

It was a three-legged dresser now. And he just kicked off another leg. Totally not the route any of us thought it would take. We thought surely, he would fix the leg. We thought maybe there would be talk of a hammer and a nail. But he just kicked off a leg and mumbled dammit. Asked for a hammer…but not for any needed repairs…and silently demolished the other two legs. It was a swift decision. But he had made up his mind.

He flipped the dresser amputee to the ground with the force of a god and stood before us proud. It was the lowest dresser I had ever seen. And he walked out of the closet.

"Oh my God! How white trash are we???" Grace was asking through unhinged laughter. "We don't fix a dresser. We just break off the other legs. How white trash are we???"

And I thought of nearly a million houses I have seen over the years with broken down buses parked somewhere in their yards. No plans to fix them. Just leave them. Right where they stalled out. We had become these people in less than 24 hours.

And we have about zero plans to buy a new dresser. It can sit closer to the ground than most furniture. And Grace will most likely retrieve her clothes hunched over like an elderly lady, but that really short dresser is staying. Right where it is. Hole in the bottom and legless glory. This is where we left it. This is where it will stay. Amen.

The Butterfly Massacre

Josh is currently a 4th grader. He is a hot mess, and I like to call him a hot potato…for really no reason other than he gets hot a lot. He's our cuddly little Panda Bear. We are so lucky all the time this happy go lucky kiddo came strolling into our crazy world. He fits right in with the rest of us, and just kind of rolls along with all the fun and all the not so fun moments in life. He is a Hooks through and through. But I will tell you, his role in life is truly the most mischievous Hooks in The Hooks House. Josh cannot be trusted.

Josh cannot ever be trusted with a secret. It's just too hard for him. He has almost unraveled many many surprises…and by almost I'm just trying to be kind…he has let the cat out of the bag numerous times. He cannot handle Christmas presents or birthday presents being in the house. He will seek them out…He will totally find them…and peak on everything…and then tell you thank you weeks before Christmas…and that he would like to just open them now please. He will scroll through your Amazon orders too and find any treat you bought him. He cannot be trusted when surprises are on the horizon. His father is actually the same way. It makes me laugh or get crazy angry. But, either way, he is this happy little panda who walks around with a smile destroying others' surprises at every turn. Whatever, Josh. Whatever. This would prove highly unfortunate, however, for Josh's 4th grade teacher. Don't worry. I got to have a LONG phone call about it.

Josh's 4th grade class has a puppet. A gorilla puppet named Ivan, to be exact. The class apparently loves this puppet. And I'm sure Josh does too. I have never actually seen this puppet, and I can't know how much it looks like a real gorilla, but I imagine it as a stuffed animal looking thing who "talks" to the class every so often. Actually, the puppet "whispers" to the teacher and she tells the class what Ivan the Gorilla Puppet has said. Pretty elaborate in the world of puppets. Maybe Ivan is a puppet who gives a life lesson. Or praise for jobs well done. Or winning lottery numbers. I can't know. But whatever the case, this puppet is held in high esteem which is a pretty great gig if you're a puppet...I mean, so many puppets just get the roll of being creepy.

Anyhoo, Josh's class was celebrating Ivan's birthday. The puppet. He had a birthday celebration in class. I can't make this shit up. This is a great life for a human, let alone a puppet. The class was going around saying everything they loved about Ivan...the puppet. The puppet y'all. He had kids talking about his accolades and attributes...and a birthday party...I mean, one lucky fucking gorilla puppet.

Now on a side note, I must tell you that Josh was standing at the front of the class. Working the technology for the morning announcements. This apparently is his daily job. I would know all this because his teacher told me every detail of this horrible puppet birthday atrocity caused by my youngest child. His position in the class is important because he is standing behind the teacher's table. And, in front of Josh...so tempting...so close...is Ivan the gorilla puppet's birthday present. Birthday present y'all. It's wrapped. The gorilla puppet Ivan is living a better life than so many gorilla puppets I am certain...oh, and humans.

And as these sweet little angels take turns saying loving words about Ivan...the gorilla puppet who is celebrating his birthday...Josh is staring at the present. Josh is looking temptation in the eye. Josh is living his best life. Working some technology early in the morning...preparing for the gorilla puppet birthday of the century...and the present...one of the things Josh loves the most...is really really close to his hands. This must have been more than he could bear.

One peak y'all. Just one. One little peak to see what Ivan...the fucking puppet...got for his birthday. It was too good to pass up. Too good. And he quickly peaked inside the box. Oh, the choices we make early in the morning that will lead to our demise when we are 10.

And in an instant, it happened. Y'all. The box was full of wind-up paper butterflies. The kind that come fluttering out to surprise people and make their hearts swell and sing. The kind that would turn a gorilla puppet birthday into one for the record books. 10-year-old students would ooh and ahh. You can feel the excitement the teacher had when she was painstakingly wrapping a box of butterflies for the gorilla puppet birthday gathering. They would soar into the air to the amazement of all around. And soar they did.

And Josh was dead. He was panic stricken. There was no little puppet t-shirt or puppet pack of cigarettes or a puppet fedora in the box...This was a once in a lifetime box of butterflies...once in a lifetime...and they came fluttering out from that one little peak. And he was at the front of the class. And he was grasping and reaching and somewhat destroying with his big bear paws the paper wind up butterflies. Trying to get them back into the box.

Grabbing. Crushing. Panicked. Sweating instantly. Heart stopping guilt. A box of fucking butterflies y'all. How could he have known? And the whole class is watching. There is no going back from this. The shock. The dismay. The massacre of so many wind-up butterflies and the birthday disappointment from Ivan the Gorilla Puppet. It was too much. It was just all too much. Let's just move to Montana because we are clearly ruined here in Buda, TX. And Ivan would probably never speak to Josh again…I mean, through his teacher to Josh again.

Surprise over. Ruined. So ruined. The students were upset. The teacher was upset. Ivan was probably crushed. And Josh stood with an open box with now motionless wind-up butterflies all over the room. Dammit all. One sneaky little peak. Who would have ever banked on wind up paper butterflies for a one-time explosion of pure panic??? Oh, the panic. When he recounted the butterfly massacre he clearly stated, "Mom. They just kept coming. And I was grabbing. And trying so hard to just make it stop." I bet, baby. I so bet you were.

I had to have a phone call conference with the teacher about Ivan's ruined birthday surprise extravaganza. I had to talk to Josh about keeping presents for puppets closed (yes, that is the weirdest sentence I have ever said). And when I think about the sheer panic and mayhem of peaking in a box and having butterflies come out…I laugh and laugh and laugh. It brings me so much joy. So much dead wind-up Gorilla puppet birthday ruined joy.

I'm a horrible person.

The Hooks Go to College

It's not every day The Hooks go to college. It happens horribly too. Partially because we love each other so damn much. Partially because there are so damn many of us. Partially because we are all running on 100 pounds of anxiety feeling all the emotions of a Bear leaving our home…ugh…Taking Jake to college was awful. I couldn't believe how much we were all intermittently crying, and how many stressful arguments you could get into late at night at a Walmart. But leave it to us to make an emotional event a little worse.

The day we were moving Jake into the dorm, we all felt like amateurs. Because we totally were. This was our absolute first rodeo. We had never had a kid leave home let alone feel the pressure of decorating his dorm room. It's so much. Plan on drinking. Plan on just going ahead and crying harder than you ever have in your life. But before that happens, if you're a Hooks, plan on maybe just maybe needing serious medical attention or causing others to think a murder has taken place.

When we walked down the hallway with bags of stuff, after fighting about 2 billion other extremely emotional families for parking, we noticed there were multiple workers directly outside of Jake's room. Like ladders right in front of his door. People literally about to hear your every argument and cuss word. Right outside. We introduced ourselves because that is who we are and what we do. Offered some polite banter before walking through that door and knowing full well they would have a front row seat to the Hooks Family Show of a Lifetime.

We got in and got organized. I think I had read that somewhere. Get organized. Give everyone a job or something to do so everyone can feel like they were part of the day. I was making a bed. Grace was organizing the bathroom. Jude was helping to unload some heavy stuff and Josh was waiting for his job. Couldn't leave him out.

Now, let me pause here and tell you that Josh is often my helper in the kitchen. He can cut up potatoes or slice up veggies…any type of fruit too…He's been my slicer and dicer for a couple of years now and I trust him in this arena. He's careful. And maybe that makes me careless, but I have taught him knife safety by default. I needed some help, and he answered the call. You can all pass a fat slice of judgement because he was 7 and using a cutting board and a large knife.

So, I handed him a paring knife and told him to be careful and open the rug packaging for me. Wow. I clearly was not firing on all cylinders at this moment. I look back at me handing a knife to a 9-year-old and telling him to cut away from himself while opening said packaging, and I honestly can't believe I'm allowed to raise children. My only excuse was my emotional state. That's all I have to explain it. But I handed the kid a knife and a packaged rug and walked away.

It took about 3.2 seconds for the screaming to start. Scream upon scream. We ran into the living space and there was blood everywhere. Josh had gashed his thumb good. Of course, he had. Of course, the 9-year-old who had recklessly been handed a knife to open an enormous package was bleeding and screaming. Corey was yelling. Jake was yelling. The whole Hooks Family lost their shit. No one was comforting Josh. We were all yelling and cussing and screaming and looking for towels and a first aid kid we knew we had packed and trying to find a damn band aid and pointing fingers galore.

Josh was screaming over and over, "Am I going to the hospital???"

"No!!!!!!" Was the resounding reply delivered at decibels that were totally unfair to anyone else living in the dorms.

I felt lucky because Jake's roommates hadn't moved in yet. I felt lucky that we were all alone. And then I remembered all the men working right outside the door…And I wanted to die just a little more than usual. Why are we always the white trash crazy family? Why are we always the ones wielding knives and making poor choices? Why are we so loud too? This is how we will all be remembered. As the really loud family with a massive propensity for inconvenient bodily afflictions.

"What the fuck were you doing with a knife Josh?" Corey yelled…Oh shit was all I could think…

"MOM gave me the knife to open the rug!!!" Josh yelled back. And I hated myself so very much.

Everyone looked at me. I could feel the astonished stares of the workers on the other side of the door who had just heard the big reveal…like the mask coming off at the end of Scooby Doo…the audience for sure would gasp.

"He's totally my potato peeler at home. And he can totally cut a veggie too." I said with fake relaxation in my voice. Like they were the crazy ones for not handing Josh knives and large packages sooner.

No one bought it. The attack was merciless. "Jesus Mom." was stated about 982 times. And the disappointed side eye from every child. Even Josh. My husband was beside himself. "What were you thinking?" Even Josh turned on me. And I was certain the guys on the other side of the door were at this point taking notes on how to ruin a dorm move in day...Hand the 9-year-old a knife would now be top on their lists. Most would think it would go without saying, but The Hooks made sure it made the tip top of the list.

Josh did not lose a thumb that day. Nor did he go get stitches. There was some glue put on it and gauze and Band-Aids and Neosporin too. We applied tons of pressure. We did all the things to get back on track in no time at all. Because we are also The Hooks. A foul-mouthed motley trashy crew of humans who will make sure a moment is worth the making, and love literally bleeds out of every minute ticking by. We are a helluva mess, but we are determined. And making Jake's dorm move in day feel complete could not have happened without some good old fashioned Hooks calamity. It's just in our blood. Or at least in the blood all over the floor from Josh's poor thumb.

Y'all. The magic is in the memories and the moments you will laugh at later. The magic is in knowing who you are as a whole family. The magic is in the making and the making of the magic is inside all of us. The Hooks are a mess. But man, we are lovable. And I think we add a little salt to this crazy life.

So, stop being embarrassed of your own personal insane clown posse. It's all those crazy animals who make life more fun. And just don't hand knives to little kids. Truly. I probably didn't even need to tell you that one…But it's on the house from all of us to all of you. Enjoy every moment. Especially the funny ones.

And we cried y'all. We cried like none of us have ever cried before. When that dorm room was complete and the day was over, we sobbed. We held each other so tight and didn't know how to say, "Goodbye". It was the longest saddest moment of my life. And I will do it again this year. I will say, "Goodbye…" to my Doodle. And then my Grace. And someday to my littlest bear too.

And those are such big hard days. Because we love each other. Because we have sat down together almost every night for decades now. Because we have yelled and screamed and laughed and cried and laughed some more. Because we are The Hooks House. And somewhere along the way we looked around and said that this was the best place on the planet earth. I cannot tell you how much it means to just have a good family you love. It means everything.

Corey and I have promised each other that on our next go round we will raise a really shitty family, so it doesn't hurt so much when they leave. We will raise shitty kids who we somewhat dislike and spend zero time together so when they leave, we don't feel like we are missing them so much. We will make each other miserable on the next go round, but this one, we really messed up big because these are my favorite people in the entire universe.

Y'all. Love your rag tag army of hooligans with everything in you. Love them. Just love them. And then love them some more. And be exactly who you are…Embrace your trashiness. Embrace your stupid idiot assholes you raised from the ground up. Embrace all your terrible moments and see the comedy gold you're living out. Don't ever wish to be some other perfect family. Perfect families don't exist. They just don't. And you and yours are absolutely wonderful just the way you are…trust me. These are the good old days.

Cheap and Easy Part II: The Recipes

I don't have many talents. It's just true. I have about three: I'm funny. I'm an incredible typist. And I can make the best Cheap and Easy Dinners. Seriously. I believe this is a talent. Ordinary people like me do not have time to make gourmet meals. Do not have money to make gourmet meals. And we are overwhelmed by words like Cumin or Zest or Marinate...We are overwhelmed by making sure things broil or making a roux. I don't even know what a roux is...I'm sure it's lovely. But what I DO know is feeding a family of six on a shoestring budget. I DO know how to make dinner in a flash or utilize a crockpot. And I DO know how to ensure everyone eats (at least kinda) because it's always yummy. If there was an Olympic event for cooking on a budget, I would be the world record gold medalist every time.

I want to share my not so fancy dinners with y'all because it's what brings my people to the table. I want you to read these recipes and think, "I can make that...". I want you to feel inspired to bring some folks together around a table and not break the bank. I am no genius, but this I know how to do...

Ok...take a deep breath. You got this. And y'all, make a menu. Mine is usually on scratch paper and it hangs on the fridge. Every Sunday is Breakfast for Dinner too. We have a solid rotation of Breakfast for Dinner items, and honestly, who doesn't like Breakfast for Dinner (except for Claire's husband, Patrick). Take the thought out of what you're making tonight. Just make a menu for one week at a time, and you will thank yourself for saving your brain power for more important things like how the hell do we pay for all the damn school pictures again this year.

Crack Chicken Sandwiches
From Jody Cook

Ingredients:

1 five-pound bag of frozen chicken breasts (you can do three pounds also)
2 blocks of cream cheese (go generic here)
1 Ranch seasoning packet
1 package bacon
1 package of hamburger buns (I buy the white bread generic 16 pack)

1. Put thawed chicken breasts, two blocks of cream cheese (set it on top of the chicken) and ranch packet on low in the crockpot for 6-8 hours.

2. Make the entire package of bacon (I cut my bacon into smaller pieces before I make it. And when I make a lot of bacon, I bake it on a cooking sheet at 425 degrees for about 20 minutes).

3. Add bacon to the crack chicken about 30 minutes before serving and shred the chicken at the last minute.

4. Put crack chicken on hamburger buns and serve warm and yummy.

I usually put these in my kids' lunch boxes too the next day.

Beef Tips on Rice
From Kay Steiger

Ingredients:

1 Package of Beef Stew Meat (I usually do the one listed as "Family Pack")
2 cans of Golden Mushroom Soup
1/2 a Stick of Butter
2 Cans of Water (fill up the soup cans)

1. Put thawed stew meat, Golden Mushroom Soup, Butter and 2 cans of water on low in the crockpot for 6-8 hours
2. Make Instant White Rice in the Microwave (I always buy the generic brand and with my family of 6 I make the whole box…I microwave for 10 minutes)
3. Serve the Beef Tips on top of the Rice.

Buffalo Chicken Sandwiches
From Jody Cook

Ingredients:

1 five-pound bag of frozen chicken breasts
1/2 a large bottle of Frank's Original Cayenne Pepper Hot Sauce
1 Ranch Packet
1/2 stick of butter
Hawaiian Rolls (Go generic here to save money)
Sliced Colby Jack Cheese (I buy the store brand for this)

1. Put thawed chicken, 1/2 a bottle of Frank's, Ranch Packet and Butter in crockpot on low for 6-8 hours

2. Shred Buffalo Chicken when finished cooking (I usually just use two forks to tear it)

3. Scoop Buffalo Chicken onto Hawaiian rolls and put a small slice of Monterrey Jack Cheese

4. Bake in the oven for 10 minutes at 350 degrees (Any leftovers go in my kids' lunches and leftover Buffalo chicken goes on top of baked potatoes when we have baked potato night)

Dr. Pepper Pulled Pork
From Meredith Walker

Ingredients:

Pork Roast or Pork Butt or Pork Tenderloin (whatever is cheapest or on sale)
Large Bottle of Sweet Baby Ray's Honey BBQ Sauce or whatever you like.
1/2 Bottle of Water (fill up the BBQ sauce bottle and shake it up)
20 Oz Bottle of Dr. Pepper
1/2 a stick of Butter
Hamburger Buns (I always go with the generic 16 pack)

1. Put thawed pork, entire bottle of BBQ sauce, 1/2 bottle of water, 20 oz Dr. Pepper, and 1/2 stick of butter in crockpot on low for 6-8 hours.

2. Shred or Chop pork when it's done.

3. Place on Hamburger Buns and Eat! Any leftover gets made into Pulled Pork Nachos or Becomes a topping for Baked Potato Night

Sweet and Spicy Pork Tacos
From Jody Cook
(And they aren't really that spicy if you have kiddos)

Ingredients:

1 Pork Roast or Pork Butt or Pork Tenderloin…Again, find what's on sale.
1 large jar of Pace Mild Picante Sauce (you can grab generic if you like)
1 bag of Brown Sugar
1/2 stick of Butter…I like Butter y'all.
Tortillas (My family likes flour, and I will do whatever brand is on sale)
Shredded Monterrey Jack
1 bag of broccoli slaw (don't be afraid of this…it's just in a bag already shredded)

1. Put thawed pork, jar of picante sauce, Brown sugar and butter in crockpot on low for 6-8 hours

2. When finished cooking shred the pork

3. Place on tortilla

4. Add shredded Monterey Jack Cheese and Broccoli Slaw

Crockpot Baked Potatoes
From Kay Steiger

Ingredients:

1 Bag of Potatoes
Cooking Oil
Salt

1. Wash potatoes and poke three fork holes in them (I poke them three times each and I have no idea why, but I always do).

2. I pat each potato with cooking oil…like I put it on my hands and then pat them with it…

3. Place them in the crockpot and sprinkle with salt and cook on low for 6-8 hours.

4. Any leftover meats we have (the pulled pork, the crack chicken, anything) goes on the table for potato toppers.

Stringer Sandwiches
From Christina Stringer

Ingredients:

Sliced ham (I do a package of it, not the freshly sliced kind from the deli because I'm poor, but a package sold in the meat department)
Sliced provolone (again, not the deli type, but go for it if your budget is different from mine)
Hawaiian Rolls (Kings Hawaiian if funds are good, the grocery store brand if it's later in the month)
Pesto (but I can't use this because Grace has a nut allergy)

1. Place ham cheese and pesto on Hawaiian roll

2. Bake in oven on 350 degrees for 10 minutes.

3. The leftovers go in my kids' lunches.

Easy Meatloaf
From My Mama

Ingredients:
3 pounds of hamburger meat (It used to be less, but everyone grew up)
Ketchup
1 egg
Two heels of bread (all my heels of bread are frozen in our freezer as soon as we finish a loaf)

1. Put thawed hamburger meat in a bowl with egg and two torn up heels of bread and ketchup…some…maybe 1/2 a cup if you want to get technical.

2. Squish together with your hands. This part sucks. Take your rings off. And it's just cold and gross-ish.

3. Pat into a square baking pan for the 3 pounder or a loaf pan if doing less than two pounds.

4. Put ketchup on top of the meatloaf.

5. Bake at 400 degrees for an hour.

Inside Out Grilled Cheese Sandwiches Created by my Shoestring Budget

Ingredients:
Heels of bread (because you've been freezing them every time you get to the bottom of a loaf of bread)
Cheese (I don't buy sliced cheddar cheese because it's more expensive. I buy a block of medium cheddar each week. We like cheese here)
Butter

*I do my grilled cheese on the George Foreman grill because it is just plain easier to make several hot sandwiches at once on a George Foreman.

1. Put butter on the inside of the heels of bread (the heel side…which is the actual outside…goes on the inside of these sandwiches so your kids can't see it and say they hate it)

2. Put slices of cheddar cheese on the sandwich.

3. Grill on the George Foreman till golden delicious.

4. I always serve these with a can of generic tomato soup and add a can of milk to the soup while cooking.

Easy Lasagna
From Rachel Browne

Ingredients:

No Boil/Oven Ready Lasagna Noodles (I thought you had to boil lasagna noodles before you baked them. Turns out you don't. There are oven ready noodles that are ready for the pan and baking.)
Spaghetti Sauce (I buy the large Prego Traditional)
1/2 Jar of Water
1 1/2 pounds hamburger meat (I buy the three-pound log of hamburger meat and cut it in half and freeze the other pound and a half)
Cottage Cheese (I get the large generic container)
Pizza cheese (the recipe I received calls for shredded mozzarella and shredded Parmesan, but that can get expensive. Most grocery stores will have "pizza cheese" which is some generic form of mozzarella and Parmesan and it's perfect and cheaper.)
1 Egg

1. Mix together browned meat, and spaghetti sauce and 1/2 jar of water (get a big bowl and a ladle to make your life easier…). This is your meat sauce.

2. In a 9x12 greased deep casserole dish, layer meat sauce then noodles and then more meat sauce (I actually buy a disposable lasagna pan because I am lazy about washing this dish.)

3. Mix the entire container of cottage cheese with the egg and use it for the next layer.

4. Layer pizza cheese, then noodles, then pizza cheese and then meat sauce.

5. Cover with foil and bake in the oven at 350 for an hour.

6. Uncover and top with more pizza cheese and cook until cheese is melted.

7. Let stand for 15 minutes before you serve.

Cheese Tortellini with Sausage
From Claire Kelly

Ingredients:

1 pound of Italian sausage (the kind in the tube and just get the store brand)
1 large bag of frozen cheese tortellini
2 cans of Italian tomatoes (go generic here…every penny counts)
1 block of cream cheese
1 small jar of marinara

1. Brown the sausage meat.

2. Put frozen tortellini, sausage, tomatoes, cream cheese and marinara in the crockpot.

Cook on low for 5-6 hours

*If you forget to put it in the crockpot, which for some reason I often do with this recipe, then you can boil the tortellini and throw the sausage, cream cheese, tomatoes and marinara in a pan and make the sauce. Then add it all together.

Hash brown Potato Soup
From Jody Cook

Ingredients:

1 bag southern style hash browns (the little squares)
1 can or carton of chicken broth (32 ounces)
1 10 oz can of cream of chicken soup (go generic here for sure)
1 block of cream cheese
Salt and pepper to taste

1. Put frozen hash browns, chicken broth, can of cream of chicken and salt and pepper into the crockpot on low for 6-8 hours.

2. Thirty minutes before it's ready, add cream cheese. You may have to cut it into cubes so it will melt better.

3. You can always add bacon and shredded cheese to top it and make it even yummier.

Spaghetti and Meatballs From My Mama

Ingredients for Meatballs:

1 1/2 pounds hamburger meat (and y'all, I always buy the tube of meat because I can't care)
1 to 1 1/2 cups quick oats
1 can of evaporated milk (generic is best here too…generic is almost always best by the way)
Flour
Salt and pepper
Spaghetti Sauce (I use Prego Traditional and get the 45oz jar)
1/2 jar of water

*I usually get two boxes/bags of spaghetti noodles for a family of 6. I am a firm believer in leftovers…My kids eat them when they get home from school and when they were younger, every Saturday we had "Leftover Lunch" and pull out every single leftover in the fridge and eat like kings. It works y'all.

1. Put hamburger meat, oats and evaporated milk in a mixing bowl and squish it all together with your hands…just go ahead and hate me for this…

2. I fry my meatballs in my electric skillet (just got a new one after the one I got when I was first married broke…over 20 years old…). I use butter to fry them in so, it is already hot and waiting for the meatballs by the time I place them in the skillet. So, this step is to say, "Turn on the electric skillet or the heat to the pan!"

3. Find a small bowl and sift flour (maybe a cup or less), salt and pepper. I don't have a sifter so, I just use a fork.

4. Roll the meatball mixture into small balls. Then coat them in the flour/salt/pepper mixture and place them in the skillet. Do this until all meat mixture is gone. You will flip them and turn them to make sure all sides get cooked.

5. Your noodles should already be cooking at this point.

6. Once your meatballs seem good and fried, Add the jar of sauce and fill it with a half jar of water to the sauce too. Do not drain the grease/fat. This makes it taste so damn good.

7. Drain the noodles when they are finished and top with the meatballs and sauce...So yummy!

Taco Meat Quesadillas
Created in My Very Own Kitchen

Ingredients:

Leftover Taco Meat (chicken or beef or pork…whatever works)
Tortillas
Shredded Cheese

* I started doing this when the kids were in Elementary. If I have leftover taco meat (chicken or pork or ground beef), I make them into quesadillas…It's a nice little Cheap and Easy solution for a random container of taco meat.

1. Line a cooking sheet with tortillas and top with shredded cheese and taco meat.

2. Add another tortilla to the top of each.

3. Bake at 350 degrees for 10 minutes. And everyone is happy. I use a pizza cutter to cut them into triangles when they are finished.

Pot Roast Enchiladas
From Me Because I was Desperate

Ingredients:

Pot Roast (About 3 to 5 Pounds)
1 Can Refried Beans
Shredded Cheddar Cheese
2 Cans of Red Enchilada Sauce (Generic Works Perfect)
Flour Tortillas (You can use corn, but my kids hate corn tortillas)

1. Cut Pot Roast into Cubes…No Need to Be Accurate…Just Making it Smaller Chunks.

2. Cook Pot Roast and both cans of Enchilada Sauce on low in the crockpot for 6-8 hours.

3. Get a nice casserole dish or something and spread the refried beans on the tortillas and line them up ready to fill (like tacos side by side).

4. Fill bean lined tortillas with the pot roast and enchilada sauce and sprinkle with the shredded cheese.

5. Roll the tortillas to make individual enchiladas.

6. Pour sauce and sprinkle cheese over the top of enchiladas.

7. Bake on 350 for ten minutes and ENJOY!

Homemade Chicken Noodle Soup Created by Me When We Were Crazy Broke

Ingredients:

1 Rotisserie Chicken Pre-Cooked from the Store
1 Bag of Egg Noodles
2 Sticks Butter
Salt and Pepper to Taste
3-4 chicken bouillon cubes

1. Bring the entire bag of noodles to boil in a pot.

2. While noodles are waiting to boil, go ahead and de-bone the chicken while putting chicken in the pot with noodles.

3. Add both sticks of butter and chicken bouillon cubes as everything is coming to a boil together.

4. Add salt and pepper to taste.

*Super simple, but super good…Use a big pot and make a ton…Yummy leftovers for days!

The Best Baked Chicken From a Million Kitchen Failures

Ingredients:

3-5 Pounds Chicken Breast
Garlic (I use a little jar of garlic)
Salt
Olive Oil

1. Preheat Oven to 450 degrees.

2. Cover the chicken in Olive Oil, Garlic and Salt.

3. Bake the chicken for 15 minutes at 450 then take it out and flip every piece over.

4. Bake the chicken again for 10 minutes at 450 then take it out and flip every piece over.

5. Bake the chicken again for 5 minutes at 450.

You can cut this chicken with a fork, and it is delicious. It's easy peasy and makes everyone happy and it makes you feel super healthy too when you put it on the table.

Crockpot Brisket
From Kay Steiger

Ingredients:

Brisket
1 Bottle of Liquid Smoke
Butter to taste

1. Place the brisket in a container that seals and empty the bottle of Liquid Smoke over the brisket.

2. Let the brisket marinate (don't be afraid of the word) in the Liquid Smoke overnight.

3. Cook in the crockpot and throw in some butter on low for 6 - 8 hours.

Barbecue enthusiasts will tell you it's cheating…And it just may be…But for a working mom this is a delicious brisket ready and waiting when you come home to dinner. By the way, you can put ribs in the crockpot too. Just ribs and a bottle of barbecue sauce and some butter. I'm sure this is cheating too.

Texas Toast Pizza
From God Knows Where

Ingredients:

Loaf of Texas Toast (Generic please and thank you)
Pizza Sauce (Just buy in the jar/can)
Shredded Mozzarella Cheese
Pepperoni/Sausage/Hamburger Meat (Whatever you got...)

1. Place the Texas Toast on a Cooking Sheet and on 425 degrees for two minutes on each side.

2. Take the toasted toast to the table and let your family build their own pizzas...Sauce, cheese, toppings and then place back on the cooking sheet.

3. Broil on high for about 1 minute. Watch it the whole time because I often mess this part up.

We have done this little dinner a bunch with extra kids when mine were little. They always think it's so fun, and honestly it's a damn good personal pizza.

Meatball Subs
From a Spark of Creativity with Meatballs

Ingredients:

Meatballs (see recipe for meatballs above in Spaghetti and Meatballs)
2 Cans Tomato Sauce
Submarine Sandwich Bread/Steak Rolls
Shredded Mozzarella Cheese

1. Make the meatballs and instead of spaghetti sauce, add tomato sauce…it's just thicker.

2. Spoon meatballs onto sub sandwich bread.

3. Top with mozzarella cheese.

I usually make frozen French fries to go with this meal or even regular potato chips. Nothing better than a hot meatball sub!

Mini Calzones
From Claire Kelly

Ingredients:

2-3 Cans Refrigerated Crescent Rolls (depending on the size of your family)
Pepperoni/Sausage/Hamburger Meat
Jar of Marinara
Shredded Mozzarella
Melted Butter (for some flare y'all)

1. Separate the crescent rolls into the precut triangles and flatten to make them bigger.

2. Fill with marinara, mozzarella and whatever meat topping you wish.

3. Fold over with the filling inside and use a fork to seal it (and it makes it look cute).

4. My husband likes to brush them with melted butter because sometimes we are extra.

5. Bake according to the crescent roll packages

I will tell you this is one of the meals we love, but it takes that added extra steps and we are always in a hurry so, this meal is a treat. Again, all leftovers go in lunches because we are lazy lunch packers.

Chicken and Rice
From the 1980's Kitchen

Ingredients:

Family Sized Can Cream of Mushroom Soup
Instant White Rice (in the box or even the boil bags…I just cut those open)
3 - 5 pounds frozen chicken breasts
Butter to taste

1. Add thawed chicken, can of Cream of Mushroom Soup, can of water, about 2-4 cups of rice depending on how much y'all like rice and a half a stick of butter on low in the crockpot for 6 hours.

That's it. The '80's weren't wrong with this one. It's tried and true. Don't forget about it. It was a favorite then and it's a favorite now. Enjoy.

Hooks Casserole
From Me When I Noticed Elbow Macaroni was Cheap

Ingredients:

One Bag of Elbow Macaroni
1 pound of Hamburger Meat
Spaghetti Sauce
One Bag of Shredded Mozzarella Cheese

1. Brown hamburger meat and put it in a casserole dish after draining.

2. Boil elbow macaroni and put in same casserole dish after draining.

3. Add spaghetti sauce and mozzarella cheese and mix.

4. Bake for 30 minutes on 350 degrees.

That's all it takes! Super easy and inexpensive and yummy. Nothing fancy but oh so good.

Breakfast for Dinner Rotation:

1. Pancake Night - We use the "Just Add Water Mix" and store brand of course. Add some chocolate chips to make it extra healthy. And if you want super yummy, reheated pancakes, then heat them up the next day in the oven for breakfast.

2. Waffle Night - My husband actually goes overboard for this and bought a Belgium Waffle Maker, and now buys expensive waffle mix...But back in the day...Just Add Water mixes were king. They usually have a recipe on the back of the box for waffles too.

3. Rhode's Cinnamon Rolls - They come in the freezer section. Yes. You will have to put them in a pan and let them thaw and rise and such. But y'all. So worth the added effort.

4. Breakfast Tacos - Scrambled eggs and bacon and salsa and queso and guacamole. Easy peasy. Cheap tortillas taste grand too. We have been buying the 22 pack of Mission flour tortillas lately. So good.

5. Breakfast on a Bun - This we got from Whataburger. So yummy. Hamburger buns (I buy the cheap, white bread, 16 pack). Then you put cheese, scrambled eggs, bacon...maybe even a sausage patty...and bake them for 10 minutes at 350 degrees.

6. Breakfast Muffins - I buy the crescent rolls in a can and shape them as best I can in a muffin tin. I beat eggs with milk and pour it into each little crescent muffin thingy and add already cooked bacon or

already cooked sausage and shredded cheese. Bake at 350 for 30 minutes.

7. French Toast - We buy the big old Texas Toast and make a boat load of French Toast. Two loaves does 6 people nicely with leftovers for days. We just heat them up in the microwave for the rest of forever.

8. Biscuits and Gravy - This is one of our famous Breakfast for Dinner menu items, however, Corey makes it and doesn't follow a recipe. All I know is we use biscuits from a can, and sausage and he makes it delicious.

We buy cheap bacon. Almost every Breakfast for Dinner comes with a side of bacon, and y'all, I cut my bacon in half. Literally. I take a pair of scissors and cut my bacon in half, so it makes more pieces. Is this crazy? Maybe. But it is what I do. Bacon is expensive and everyone in our house loves it so, I started cutting it in half about four years ago, and for some strange reason, it just works.

All of our breakfast for dinners go into Tupperware or Ziplock bags. They are then our breakfast staples for the rest of the week or after school snacks. Train your family to eat a leftover for breakfast`. You will thank yourself later.

The Sides Make the Meal
*And I do Cheap and Easy with those too…

When you are cooking for a family of six and you are a full-time high school teacher, welp, you are at the mercy of the almighty clock and the ever-present dollar. I like my table to be full. I like my family to feel like they ate a meal. This makes me feel good. Not about being a mom or as a person, but it's my way of saying, "I love you," to my people. I learned how to cook at the age of 34. I am not a chef. I am not a foodie. I am an ordinary person who just keeps finding ways to put yummy food on the table in no time flat mostly because I use a crockpot and have a few wonderful side dishes as my staples…And a couple of tricks up my sleeves I've learned along the way. But honestly, quite often, the sides make a meal 10 million times better…

1. Always have a stash of "steamable" veggies in your freezer. I buy grocery store brand, and my kiddos are fans of broccoli, corn, peas and corn on the cob. I cook these all in the microwave and usually it takes about 4 1/2 minutes. Throw some butter and maybe a little salt in the dish and they get eaten up.

2. Each week I buy 3 to 4 salad kits. Again, I buy the grocery store brand because it saves at least a dollar a bag, if not more. Anyone can throw these together. All you need is scissors and something to mix with…I pour them in a big bowl and feel good about having a salad at dinner. My staples are always Cesar Salad and this amazing little Chile Lime Crunch I'm addicted to from H-E-B (if you don't live in Texas and have

H-E-B I'm just sorry). And literally, if I have to chop vegetables, I will hate everyone.

3. Put fruit on the table. I'm not ashamed to say that I have thrown a bunch of bananas on the table and called it a side dish. I love watermelon because it's Cheap and Easy (except for the cutting mess). I usually do precut fruit which costs more, but I'm also typically racing against time to get it all on the table so kids can do homework or go in a million directions.

4. A can of beans is pretty grand too. Refried. Charro. Baked. Ranch Style. It's never expensive to grab a can of beans. It can make nachos a little tastier. Or meatloaf even better. And they just won't break the bank.

5. I will also roast vegetables on 450 degrees for about 15 minutes. Green beans with garlic salt and olive oil. Brussels Sprouts with garlic salt and olive oil. Potatoes with garlic salt and olive oil. You name it. You don't have to reinvent the wheel. Garlic salt and olive oil over veggies cut up and roasting on a cooking sheet feels fancy. And it's so easy.

6. Bread. We love a roll over here. Or the fresh bread from the bakery section of the store. It's often less than $2. But listen y'all, I'm not opposed to freezing leftover hamburger or hot dog buns and making salt and pepper bread. You just thaw it and cover it in butter, salt and pepper. Pop it in the oven and bake it on 350 degrees for 10 minutes. It's delicious and you're just using your leftover frozen bread. Easy peasy.

7. If I'm baking chicken or making a meatloaf, it is Cheap and Easy to make mashed potatoes. Even the instant mashed potatoes are delicious.

8. Rice is easy too. I don't ever boil it. I cook it rice in the microwave…the boil in bag kind. My kids put their veggies on their rice. Generic white rice is one of the least expensive items to put on your table.

9. And let me never forget Mac-n-Cheese. We buy it in the four pack, and it's devoured at our house. It's just something everyone loves. It goes with burgers or hot dogs or whatever you want. Your people will eat it, and it takes nearly no time to make. It graces my table at least once a week. We even have a nickname for it: "mackers".

10. There is a recipe on the internet for Lawry's Creamed Corn. It is the best stuff ever. It's a treat at our house when I make it, but it honestly takes no time at all. Look it up. Buy the heavy whipping cream and thank yourself later. Literally. Your whole family will love you forever. Or you'll be the hit at the potluck.

11. Don't shy away from the side of pasta. Just any pasta. Make it. Butter it. Put it on the table.

Treats on Hand

I have found being able to whip up a homemade treat (or a semi homemade treat…or hell just opening a box of Twinkie's) makes everyone in my house feel like life is grand. This helped a ton when the kids were little, but to be completely honest, it still helps now. We have so many teenagers eating dinner at our house. And let's not forget all the "parties" as our children are going through school. If I have a solid stash of the basics, I can usually pull something together to add for the Teacher Luncheon, random Government class potluck, the work Christmas dinner or hey, there are 78 humans eating at my house tonight let's feed them something. I have found over the past nearly 20 years having things I can bake on the fly is a treat and treats are important. I highly suggest the following…

*Let me say here there are things you should always have on hand…Flour, Sugar, Baking Soda, Baking Powder, Eggs, Cooking Oil…These are the foundation for a million recipes. Keep them. You can go to the intermediate level and add coco, vanilla and brown sugar too…But these few inexpensive grocery items in your cabinet or fridge make a huge difference. Just buy them. Save yourself a trip to the store. Have them ready to go.

1. Maybe we all learned this during the Covid world's longest years ever but freeze your bananas and always have the stuff to make banana bread. Years ago, I found a recipe online for banana bread. There are a million out there too. But freeze your brown bananas. Have salt and flour and sugar and baking soda and eggs on hand. And get yourself a loaf pan

please while you're at it. This is for all the moments you have to say, "Oh shit", and make something for the potluck lunch or for the 88 kids you have at your house or for breakfast on the weekend. Just make banana bread. It's tried and true. Life is hard. Banana bread won't fail you.

2. Homemade brownies. I found a recipe for these when my kids were little. Yes. It takes longer than a box mix for sure, but if you just have the same ingredients lying around (flour, salt, sugar, baking soda, eggs and add some coco) you can throw these together on a whim and not have to run to the store. It's a treat on hand. You just make them at a moment's notice and your people will love them. I mean, who doesn't love a brownie? I use a recipe titled, "Mmmm Mmmmm Better Brownies" which I look up online every time.

3. Cake Cookies. A box of generic white cake mix costs about a dollar. Generic chocolate chips don't cost much either. I learned about this from a lady who was in her 70's. I was a young ish mom, and she said they were the easiest and cheapest chocolate chip cookies to make…Not the world's greatest…but they would totally do in a pinch. I used to always keep white cake mix on hand just for this…There are tons of cake cookies recipes online now, but here is the simple version:

Cake Cookies
(From a Friend Who Was Much Older and Wiser)

Ingredients:

1 box white cake mix
2 eggs
1/2 cup of oil
Chocolate chips

Preheat the Oven to 350.
Mix everything in a bowl.
Bake for 10 minutes.

Easy and delicious every single time! I add crushed Oreos sometimes too. And it was the first thing my kiddos learned how to bake on their own.

4. Those popsicles that come in the red mesh bag. You know the ones. They are in plastic sleeves, and they come in all sorts of flavors and the green ones are always leftover for like a year. Buy them in the summer. Buy them all summer. Keep them in your freezer. I pulled out all the leftover lime green ones yesterday and gave them to some kiddos and literally I think I won an award.

5. Rice Krispie Treats. That is all that needs to be said.

6. Instant drink mixes. I buy peach tea lately. Add water. And it's just delicious. Not fancy. My family just likes it in the fridge. I buy store brand, and it stays in my

pantry. This is not brain surgery. It just makes life a little better.

7. Jello. Oh my gosh. Jello. It never gets old.

8. I keep super cheap frozen pizzas at all times. I have no shame. If it's a Saturday and people are at my house…frozen pizza…I will make it for anyone. And then I put the leftovers in a bag and people can pack it for lunch. Or if you're a teenager, you will come into my room at 1am eating cold frozen pizza you found in the fridge and talk to me about life.

9. Frozen waffles are always a hit too. My people put peanut butter and jelly on them. They are always in my freezer, and they don't cost an arm and a leg if you buy store brand. They don't have to just be breakfast.

10. This may sound ridiculous, but I always "plate" my leftovers. By that I mean, I put the leftover crack chicken on buns and put them in Tupperware in the fridge. I put my leftover pulled pork on buns and put that in the fridge. I put all the hot dogs on buns and put them in the fridge too. Whatever leftover sandwiches need to be put together and put in the fridge, I do it. Here's why: if it is made into a sandwich my people will eat it like it's grab and go. If I leave it in the bowl or have buns in the pantry and the meat in the fridge, welp, they just can't seem to make it into a meal or a snack. If I take that extra step of putting it together then they will all get eaten. It doesn't seem like this would change the outcome of leftovers, but this is all it takes at my house.

11. Make homemade whipped cream. It's just heavy whipping cream and sugar. Start with two cups of cream and a cup of sugar. Get out your hand-held mixer, and you're golden. Throw this on top of instant hot coco (which we buy by the boxful). Put it on instant pudding. Heck, eat it out of the bowl. It takes like all of 32 seconds. And it's a treat. And treats seem to make life just a little sweeter.

12. Queso and chips. Queso and chips is the best ever for a treat whenever. I keep the kind you have to heat up in the microwave. No making it. Just heating it. Generic tortilla chips on hand too. If folks show up, you just heat it up. And maybe you put it in a bowl. Maybe you don't. Depends on the level of friendship to be honest.

13. Popcorn. I buy microwave popcorn by the boxful. Just like to have it around for a snack or TV or a movie or another day of other people's offspring that hang out in my living room.

14. Honey Buns. We buy them, put them on a cooking sheet with a little pat of butter on them and bake them on 350 for ten minutes. I used to think if I had a sleepover at my house, I had to run out and buy donuts for everyone. And y'all, the older they get, the more expensive this is…So, I started buying two or three boxes of honey buns for sleepovers. And no one has complained yet.

15. Martha White Muffins. This is a breakfast treat. They are so inexpensive, and everyone is excited to wake up to blueberry or chocolate chip or mixed berry muffins. A winner every single time.

16. Homemade Crockpot Hot Coco. I make this when the weather gets cold. It's part of any Christmas party and has been a staple at Grace's January birthday party. It's simple to make, and beyond delicious. I use all my Christmas mugs with it and set out some Peppermint Schnapps for the adults to make it a little more festive! I always double the recipe too and put the leftovers in Tupperware in the fridge for later...assuming there are ANY leftovers. I have sent this recipe to anyone who has asked, because you should be the star of your Christmas party too!

Crockpot Hot Coco

Dump all of this in a Crockpot on low.
1.5 cups heavy whipping cream
1 14 oz can of sweetened condensed milk
6 cups milk
1 teaspoon vanilla
2 cups milk chocolate chips

Again, I always double this recipe and it takes about 2 hours to get it all good and melty and you have to be willing to stir it too. But it is so dang yummy and worth it.

17. Pumpkin Bread is just as easy as Banana Bread. When the recipe calls for "fresh pumpkin" I just throw in a can of pumpkin...no one has time to get fresh pumpkin out of a pumpkin.

18. And don't forget about a good old cake mix and frosting. My family loves a yellow cake mix with chocolate icing...And most other humans do to. If you get the store

brand, you're going to spend less than $5 on the whole thing. And just so you know, it doesn't have to be a birthday party to have a cake. We are all old enough to know there is no need to have a party in order to make a cake...cake is a party enough.

19. Pumpkin Chocolate Chip Cookies. A can of pumpkin and a bag of chocolate chips and I typically have the rest of the ingredients. I love this recipe more than you can know, and so do my friends and family and a million teachers over the years. I have been making this recipe since 2011, and they are always completely eaten almost instantly.

Pumpkin Chocolate Chip Cooks From Amy Smith

Ingredients:

1 cup canned pumpkin (I actually use the whole can...it makes cake like cookies)
1 cup white sugar
1/2 cup vegetable oil
1 egg
2 cups all-purpose flour
2 teaspoons baking powder
2 teaspoons ground cinnamon
1/2 teaspoon salt
1 teaspoon baking soda
1 teaspoon milk
1 tablespoon vanilla
2 cups chocolate chips

Preheat oven to 350 degrees

1. Combine pumpkin, sugar, vegetable oil, and egg in a mixing bowl and set aside.
2. Combine flour, baking powder, ground cinnamon and salt (I use a fork to sift it)
3. Dissolve the baking soda with the milk (I do this in a coffee mug) and add to the pumpkin mixture.
4. Add flour mixture to pumpkin mixture, and then add chocolate chips and vanilla.
5. Bake on 350 for 12 minutes (I make little spoonful cookies)

*This is one of my most involved recipes and the baking soda and milk chemistry experiment felt way out on a limb for me at first, but I will tell you it's not hard…Just follow the recipe and know that your people will love them.

None of these things are difficult or fancy. None of the treats on this list take much time at all. But sometimes, when your bank account hurts to look at, you can still pull something together. You can still make people smile. And maybe you already know all of these things, but I'm serious when I say, these have made hard days into better days. And I don't really care what anyone thinks about my simple saving graces. These are the treats I go to. These are the things I can do when I can't exactly make ends meet. I have no time for more than this level of awesome...But you know what, over the years, this level of awesome has proven tried and true.

Don't be overwhelmed by feeding your people. I cannot say this enough, don't be overwhelmed. I am not a person who is ever going to make a recipe requiring too much of my time. I don't have it in me. I will hate everyone by the time it's finished. But I like to sit down with my family and share a meal. I like to hear about their day. I like to laugh with them. I like to have extra kids in extra chairs pulled from other rooms. As we have been living this life, "I can't" was not an option anymore. Release yourself from having to make something amazing...save that shit for Thanksgiving...I'm telling you; you can do this.

These are just some lackluster things I put on my table, and y'all, people happily eat them. This is just an easy way to fill bellies and make dinner a super joy filled experience. I am not rich. I am just an ordinary human who is constantly doing the best she can. And please, don't discount Stove Top. It's delightful. People want to put it in their mouth. You don't have to be fancy or "bougie" to make a meal. You can put good food on your table and surprise yourself with the way it makes everyone say thank you...Yep...they say thank you. And then you force them to do the dishes. It's all perfect.

And truly, if you're making gourmet meals for your family, more power to you. But you are living in a different category than me and a lot of people I know. And for a long time, I thought people who spent hours upon hours in their kitchen were better family members than I could ever be in my lifetime. But it's just not true. It just means they have more time or money than I do. Or they want to spend their time and money in a different way than I can. This does not make them good or bad. It just means we are not following the same recipes when we make a meal.

I just honestly do not want another person to fall into the same trap of thinking they are less than because their recipes require a can of soup or only three ingredients or a crockpot. Love your people. Fill their bellies. Make them laugh at the dinner table. It's all you need.

Part III Cheap and Easy: Ordinary Life Hacks

I wake up every day at 4ish. I hit snooze 982 times some days, but for the most part, my eyes are open and ready for the world by 4:30AM. There was a time in my life where I would have told you this was a holy thing. I would have told you I spent time in quiet prayer for my friends and family. And sometimes I do. But mostly, it is my one time each day I get to be alone. No one else up. And I drink coffee, do dishes and laundry, take a shower, sit on my front porch swing, scroll through Facebook, pack forgotten lunchboxes and do not speak to anyone. It's lovely. I love this part of my day. Just me and the dogs. And I couldn't ask for anything more. I have searched up "Happy Playlists" a million times on Spotify so I can have the perfect start to my day as often as possible. It's important. And I am grateful.

There are a lot of sad stories to tell. Everyone has a sad story or ten to tell. But at this moment in my life, I just want to be happy. I just want to celebrate every single day. I want to laugh and feel good. I want to be with the people who make me feel that kind of daily good. And I want to recognize the hope along the way on this crazy ordinary journey.

I think for so many of us, difficult times are just difficult. They are horrible and they are hard, and they threaten to take us under. And that's true. We are often drowning in the middle of our daily lives…But hope always seems to find us. Not some holy hope. Just daily ordinary hope. For me, honestly, it might be petting my dogs in the morning...finding a quarter on my way into work...laughing with my coworkers about ridiculous shit...the right song at the right time...good coffee...enough frozen bananas...making the whole schedule work with four kiddos...just little ordinary moments of hope that keep me smiling...keep reminding me that life is good.

We talk about this hope inside our family. These are the car ride inspirational talks. The talks where you have a kid or a partner or a friend one on one, and you get to share a little hope from the road. Your captive audience in need of a motivational speech. You see the moment, and you launch because the older we get, the more we realize moments aren't for the missing. And there are little hints that life can still be good even when it is hard.

In my life, outside of food and cheap easy dinners, there have been so many things keeping us afloat. Keeping the budget intact. I want you to have all of those ideas in your head...all of these tools in your tool kit so you can keep on keeping on. This is no little thing to find ways to make it all work. And I don't want anyone to miss out on them. I want you all to know there are a million little things making this crazy family run. And, honestly, I hope this helps you find a little peace in knowing you're just not alone in the hustle. And the hustle looks sometimes like juggling knives on fire, but if I can help you find some relief then my life is just a little better.

Hooks Family Christmas

About five years ago, we came up with our own family Christmas tradition. It's my favorite ever ever ever. We were all part of the initial planning, and I can tell you, it is one of those things we look forward to every year. We have warned our kids their future partners must be the type who can hang with this family tradition…or they don't make the cut…it's important. It makes up the fabric of who we have become as The Hooks House.

We pick a day sometime after Christmas. Usually, the 27th or 28th. When all the festivities are done and settled. And then we gather at the dinner table ready for our perfect time just for us. Each name goes into a bowl. Mom, Dad, Jake, Jude, Grace and Josh written on little slips of paper and folded nicely. Then the sections of Walmart go into a separate bowl. Kitchen, Bedroom, Pet Supplies, Toys, Electronics, Clothing, Sporting Goods…you name the section, and we write it on little slips of paper folded neatly in a bowl. Then each person draws a name (and it can't be their own name) and a section of the store. Jake might draw Josh and the Automotive section. Corey might draw Grace and the Outdoor Living section. And we are handed $10 each to buy that person a present in that particular section.

When we get to Walmart, we each set a timer on our phone for 15 minutes and away we go. Running through the store. Mostly trying to get funny items or maybe something good, but the task is always a challenge. We separate. We run into each other. Someone is in charge of Josh. We take videos that are hysterical. We look like insane people especially when the 15-minute timers go off.

And since Christmas traditions always come with a dinner option, we let everyone pick the fast food of their choice. We head home with Whataburger, Panda Express, Double Daves Pizza, Taco Bell and maybe even KFC. All jammed into one car. Which doesn't happen often anymore. Don't worry, we all argue at least 8 times.

We sit around the table and eat our subpar delicious food and give each other our gifts. And we laugh. And that for me is perfect. It took us about 20 years of marriage before coming up with this fantastic Hooks Family Christmas. It took us almost two decades to nail something we all look forward to because it is the epitome of who we are…cheap, a little crazy and in love with our family. And each year I love that night the most because we are not a perfect family, but we are a good family. We are irreverent, but somehow, we are completely wholesome. Somehow, we are everything I never even dreamed possible…a group of people who love each other and know each other and love what we know.

So, let me encourage you, your family traditions don't have to be filled with meaning and big words and fanfare. They don't have to be filled with million dollar presents either. They can just be good. Just really really good. And make you laugh and feel like you were dropped into the perfect place in the universe too. Love your family just as they are…your little family that lives in your house…and circle in tight and laugh together at Christmas…oh and totally eat Taco Bell…it's so worth it.

Family Birthday Dinners

So many traditions we have in our family exist because we were broke. We have a family of 6 so going out to dinner on a kiddo's birthday is not an option. I mean, if we do fast food, it costs upwards of $60…and that is not ok in this house. Easier to cook. Cheaper to cook. This used to stress me out. I am not even sure why anymore. But it used to stress me out that we didn't go out to eat to celebrate a birthday. But somewhere along the way, the realization was simple: A birthday celebration is literally just about saying, "We are so glad you are with us on this planet at this time and in this family." And we came up with a celebration we can totally make happen no matter if we are living large or scraping by.

When it is your birthday in The Hooks House, we pick a night of the week when every member will be home. And you get to pick the meal. Every detail. You are encouraged to choose your favorite foods and drinks…whatever they may be…They don't have to match either. So, we have had lasagna and garlic bread and creamed corn and strawberries. We have had French Toast and chocolate milk and peas. We have had steak and potatoes and French fries and watermelon. You name it, we make it. It's your special meal. Go for everything that makes you happy. And the kids will take sometimes a week to put their menu together.

When we sit around the table eating the most random side dishes, Corey and I will tell the story of the day you were born. We always try to tell little details we haven't ever told before…maybe something about a nurse, or something about the drive home or thoughts we had. And when it is Jake's birthday only Corey and I have the tale to tell…But when we get to Josh's birthday, everyone has a story. Everyone remembers that day. And it is the way to say, "We celebrate you." And it doesn't cost a fortune.

The big finale of the evening is Corey's Texas Chocolate Sheet Cake. He has perfected it over the years and makes it 100% from scratch…even the icing. And we stand around and sing Happy Birthday with the lights off so the candles show.

And that is it y'all. Nothing fancy. Just some people who love you telling about one of the best days of their entire lives. The day you were born. And it is beyond special because it is just us remembering you.

Please give yourself some space to just be together. To just celebrate together. To tell the stories no one else knows. To remind your people that the day they were born changed the Universe and made our family better. It can be that easy.

E salon

OK…I dye my hair. I have for years upon years. And I have super long hair too. I am not a natural red head, and I love that most people think I am. And I have had 9 million folks tell me to not dye it and let my gray show…But I am not there yet. I may never be. I might be 98 years old with a long crown of bright red hair because it makes me feel good.

However, over the years, I have had to give up dying my hair at times because it is so expensive. I quit going to a salon over 10 years ago and started using box dye. This was an adventure in orange hair quite often. I could never find a good match, and things just got weird.

And then one day, a random conversation in my front yard led me to Esalon. It is an online company with colorists there to help you get the perfect hair color for YOU. You fill out a form, send in a picture of you, and a picture of what you want your hair color to look like. They correspond with you and ask you questions...And THEN...this is the big part...They mail you salon grade color straight to your mailbox!!!! What??? You can set it to come every 6 weeks, 8 weeks or just whenever you need it...It's amazing. And so easy. And it's not expensive when you compare it to going to a salon. Less than $30. And did I mention it comes to your mailbox???

I usually change the color a bit for summer or fall via their website. It has never been difficult. And my husband has become my beautician. We set up in the kitchen and make the hair magic happen. I cannot begin to explain to you the convenience of it all. I have been using Esalon for over five years now...maybe more...and it is the best thing ever. I highly encourage you to check it out.

I think sometimes when times are tight, we give up on the things that make us feel good. And I get that...I understand why so many of us cut our own hair and do our own nails...I don't have the money to spend. I just don't have it. But being able to color my hair...y'all it means so much to me...I might be shallow...I don't care...long red hair makes me smile and smile. We work so hard for the other humans in our lives to have their wants and needs met, but this one thing is just for me. It has been so worth it.

Afterpay

I think it was the summer of 2021 when my friend, Cassell, told me about Afterpay. We were on a walk, and she referenced it and I had no clue what she was talking about. If you're like me and grew up broke in the 1980's, you remember Layaway. It was at every big store…JCPennys, Edisons, Montgomery Ward, KMart…And it was the way your mom did Christmas and birthdays. Things went on Layaway. And you paid them off little by little. It was brilliant. You had a final due date too. No interest. No hidden fees. Just time for you to make sure everyone got what they wanted and needed for Christmas.

This went away at some point in time. I have no idea if there are any major stores out there still offering layaway, but I haven't heard of it or seen it in a long, long time. And then Afterpay. This day with my friend changed the way I shop for clothes for my family. It's glorified layaway, and I believe it caught on during Covid.

Afterpay is an app I have on my phone. There are tons of shops on there…Under Armour, Lulu Lemon, Old Navy, Urban Outfitters, Pandora, Carter's, PacSun…so many stores. And you can make a purchase, they ship it to you, and you pay for it in four payments. One a month. Until it is paid off. It comes right out of your checking account.

We have bought school clothes this way. Jeans. Shoes. And my teens use it too. To get the things they want and then pay them out. There is no credit check. And you can always pay it off early. But for a family needing to do Christmas or birthdays, Afterpay can be a beacon of hope.

I'm sure there are people who would tell you it's silly to pay things off in four payments. I'm sure there are folks who might look down on this little gem. But I am here to tell you, it's worth it to at least check it out. The Hooks House has been very satisfied with our Afterpay experience. And you get reminders via text when you're about to have to make another payment. I will keep using this app forever. And honestly, I hope this helps you buy someone something special. Because there are times in my life that having the special gift makes my whole soul happy.

School Supplies

Every year this insanity hops into my life. Some people love it and get so excited about it. Some people send me texts when school supplies are back in stock in the stores. I get anxiety. We have a lot of people to buy school supplies for…It's a lot of folks who need 982 binders with brads and pockets and sharpened pencils and all the things. Here is the honest to goodness truth about The Hooks House and school supplies: We recycle so much of them…

We have a box at the bottom of our art closet which is full of school supplies. I ordered composition books on Amazon when there was a deal once and those still exist. We recycle binders and notebooks and folders from the years before. We tear out pages and use them again because I cannot spend hundreds of dollars on school supplies each year.

We recycle lunch boxes too. I mean, Josh, the 9-year-old, gets a new lunch box each year. But we have a basket with lunchboxes in it and we just keep using them until they die. Older kids don't care as much. And they will pack their lunches in almost anything so I can't stress over this any longer.

We have a shelf of a million reusable water bottles. And all the things. We do the absolute best we can with everything we already have to ease this burden which comes every August. And my kids will learn to use and reuse. It sounds lovely. It sounds ecofriendly, but it is all about costs. And my kids will be just fine…or not even notice…if they have some leftovers. Leftovers are lovely.

Also, if you want to be super wonderful, send your leftover school supplies to a high school teacher. I have a shelf in my classroom filled full of leftover binders and notebooks and pens and pencils. It is always completely empty by the end of the school year. Desperate teens who did not do a project will gladly grab from it. And a teacher will never say no to extra school supplies. I promise.

All this to say, use your leftover school supplies wisely and at the end of a school year, clean out backpacks and put stuff away in a box. Grab from it first the next year. You will thank yourself later. Honest.

At Home Birthday Parties

I love a birthday. I do. I love to celebrate and get excited, and make you feel loved through a birthday party. But I cannot always do the awesome destination birthday parties. We have done them. Sometimes in the past we have been able to throw a party at a jumpy place or somewhere it is all done for you...And those days are beautiful because...well they just are so dang easy. However, those days are mostly gone in this house just to save some money. And at home birthday parties have been some of the most fun we have ever had.

I typically google "fun birthday parties for teens", and just let the wheels start turning. We were given a projector and a screen a few years ago from my parents for Christmas so, clearly, we have done many outdoor movie nights complete with microwave popcorn and chairs set up outside. We like a good piñata too. Which always makes for a treat. But I am going to share with you the best of the best...my personal favorites sticking in my memory as the cheapest and the absolute most fun.

When Jake turned 14, we threw him a Scavenger Hunt birthday party. It was a blast. We broke the guests into teams and gave them matching bandanas to signify which team they were on. There was a list of about 30 challenges each team had to complete in 25 minutes. And one person on the team had to film on their phone as well for proof. I enlisted the help of about five other moms to be drivers for each team.

But here is where it got really good...We called our local Cabella's (sporting/hunting/outdoor store) and asked if we could bring about 35 teens to their store for a 25 minute scavenger hunt to run around and go crazy in their fine establishment. We promised them moms would be there to keep it under control a bit. And the manager thought it was a great idea. And it was 100% free.

Those kids had to do a cartwheel in the store, get a cashier to sing "Baby Got Back", find a boat and all get in it and sing "Row Row Row Your Boat…", play Duck Duck Goose in the elevator, fit as many people as possible in a tent and the list went on and on. There was a million pounds of laughter. It was so perfect.

When we returned to our house, we watched the videos the kids had made on our TV and awarded the team who had completed all challenges (or the most challenges) with lottery tickets. Because scratch off tickets are always cheap and fun. And it goes down in history as one of my favorite birthday parties I have ever thrown in my entire life.

Next on my list is the year Jude turned 14. We taped about 6 Twister boards together in our yard and told all the kiddos to wear swimsuits so they could get wet and messy. On each dot on the twister board was shaving cream dyed with Tempra paint. A regular, yet enormous, twister board with shaving cream everywhere. I called out all the plays…right hand blue, left foot red…and watched as kids slipped and slid and laughed and were insanely messy. It was a hysterical event. And so easy. Biggest expense was the Twister boards.

We had a cooking party once for Grace's birthday. I made a bunch of vanilla cupcakes and had watched a simple YouTube video showing how to make them into bears. We had tables set up in our kitchen with a bunch of little girls making cupcakes. It was easy. Let me say that again…I just made the cupcakes on my own. Then the cupcakes were their party favors. We also made chef hats out of bulletin board border and tissue paper. A little bit of stapling, but they were so cute. I think I even used the tissue paper I already had saved in my closet. I mean it was so inexpensive. It just took a little planning.

We did PJs and Pancakes for a morning birthday party…just something out of the norm. The guests came over at 9am in their pajamas (which for someone reason little kiddos always think is fun), and we made pancakes. So, some "Just Add Water" pancake mix, syrup, butter and kids in pjs. Easy peasy. And the party was over at 11am. It was beyond perfect. And you weren't spending all day getting ready for a party. You just had breakfast and played with a group of friends to celebrate you…And it was lovely.

This past year we did a karaoke party for Josh's 10th birthday. Two karaoke mics bought at Wal Mart and some shiny curtains from Target…the kind that make a "photo backdrop" for $5 each. We hooked up Spotify on our TV and hit the "Show Lyrics" button, and it was instant karaoke. 10-year-olds aren't often shy and haven't learned to only sing if they sing good so, it was a free for all. They sang. They danced. All in front of the shiny curtain with Spotify lyrics posted on our TV…It was so fun and hysterical.

We did a Nerf battle at a park one year too. Every kid brought their Nerf guns, and we bought a bunch of bullets on Amazon. We broke the kids up in teams and at the very very end we did "every man for himself". It was epic. And it even rained on the kids. They loved that part too.

The magic is in the fun. Not in the money. Just get a little creative with what you have…you'll be surprised how far it can go.

Don't be afraid to make a bunch of corn dogs or hot dogs too. You don't have to order a million pounds of pizza. Kids will eat frozen pizza too and love it. We usually make a big container of lemonade or buy the Hugs drinks that come 40 to a box. And Walmart has the cheapest party plates, napkins and such. Kids just want to have fun. They just want to feel welcomed and liked so, you serving a bag of pizza rolls is grand.

We also just started making homemade birthday cakes. Nothing fancy. No need to spend all your cash on a cake that looks like a piece of art. Just buy a box of cake mix and ice it…maybe add sprinkles if you're feeling crazy. Candles still get blown out, and kids still sing happy birthday…I found at some point I was buying things for other parents to see or out of some guilt. Kids don't care. I promise. You can always go with root beer floats too. Why not? Generic root beer is CHEAP and a bucket of the off-brand ice cream goes a long way.

You guys don't keep up with your neighbors or the kids at school for birthday parties. You just don't have to do this to yourself. Just have fun. Just invite people into your home and have fun. This is about celebrating your child, not about winning the award for most expensive birthday party ever thrown. Take some pressure off. And I promise they will remember you loved them…not what their cake looked like.

Have A Cheap Party Drink

The Hooks are party people. We have a few annual parties we throw every year. New Years Eve and an Adult Easter Egg Hunt (total blast where adults hunt for eggs at night, and man they are competitive). About five years ago we started making a big batch of our signature party drink, Beergaritas. We are tequila people, so it works for us. And it screams Texas Party. We put it in a big container for our guests, and I swear people look forward to it.

Beergaritas
(Recipe from Jody Cook)

1 can of limeade (I buy the generic frozen kind at whatever grocery store)
1 can of cheap tequila (and I mean super cheap)
2 beers (we splurge for Corona Extra usually)
A little Sprite

We use this same formula to make enough to serve lots of people. It's super easy, and I'm never going to rent a margarita machine or have some awesome open bar. But Beergaritas. They are what folks expect when they come to a party at The Hooks House, and they are pretty loved and adored.

You don't have to do Beergaritas, but I will tell you, if you like to have people at your house, make your life a little simpler and come up with an easy drink. You don't have to supply enough beer for an army or buy wine for days. You can just throw your signature drink together. Electric lemonade is easy too. It's just lemonade and cheap champagne. And it's a little different than a mimosa. Don't reinvent the wheel every time you want to have a gathering at your house. I had a friend who used to always make Sangria with grape soda and cheap wine…And we all loved it. Just come up with something that doesn't break the bank and doesn't take all of your mental power to plan.

If you ever make it out to Buda, TX and find yourself at The Hooks House, I'll make a batch of Beergaritas, and you will be glad I did.

Hooks Family Birthday Present

When my three oldest were in elementary school, it felt like every weekend there was a multitude of birthday parties. We were juggling going to close to four a weekend at times and it was overwhelming financially. My kiddos always wanted to go to the store to pick out gifts for their friends…and little kids don't consider money…so it was a battle…I think I said 9 million times, "I am not buying the $55 lego for a kid in your class!" And it felt so stressful.

I was complaining about this to another friend with lots of kids, and she gave me the greatest idea…come up with the Hooks Family Birthday Present. She had done this in her family, and their family birthday present was simple: If a friend was turning 7, they received 7 one-dollar bills, 7 quarters, 7 dimes, 7 nickels and 7 pennies…This went for any age…Not too much money and no need to take your kid to the store to pick it out. Her family birthday present was loved by all the kids. What 7-year-old doesn't want all that money???

So, I racked my brain and came up with something I could easily run into a store and grab. The Hooks Family Birthday Present for years was a six pack of mini sodas, a box of "movie" candy (the kind that is about a dollar) and a $10 gift card to Target. Easy Peasy. And of course, kids loved receiving it. This is what we were giving our friends. No questions asked. And the bickering and the long mornings in the store in the toy aisle were over.

The idea behind picking a family birthday present that you give to everyone is about low stress, time management and not murdering your child in the middle of Walmart because they are begging to buy some random kid a $75 video game. I just couldn't handle it at all anymore. And this made birthday party shopping a breeze. I hope you pick one out for your family too. Nothing too fancy. Nothing too complicated. Just something quick and seamless for you to grab. Enjoy all the stress-free present-ing in your future.

Folding Fitted Sheets

There was this time…long long ago…when I tried to fold fitted sheets and put them in some sort of linen closet. And I just ended up with a crumbled mess of crap. So, my advice to you when it comes to folding fitted sheets. Just don't.

When you have a sheet set, take one of the pillowcases. Open the pillowcase wide. Shove the flat sheet, fitted sheet and other pillowcase inside the wide-open pillowcase. Store it at the top of your closet or wherever the hell you want. Your sets stay together. Your mind stays intact.

You're welcome.

Mason Jars

Mason Jars make any gift cuter. When we had 8 million children of our own having to go through the yearly "Teacher Appreciation Week", I would honestly feel so completely stressed. A lot of folks will tell you not to care. However, your kid is the one who didn't get to bring something when the majority of other kiddos did bring something. I hated that feeling as a kiddo. And it makes me too happy to participate with crazy crap. And it makes my kids happy and their teacher happy which is a nice bonus for me. During this time when I had literally dozens of teachers to buy for, I started using Mason Jars.

I would buy big bags of candy and put them in Mason Jars with ribbon around them. Cheap and Easy. I would put school supplies in them like paper clips or rubber bands which come a million to a package. I would put lottery tickets in them. One year it was homemade sugar scrub. Whatever it was, when it was packaged in a Mason Jar, it just looked ten thousand times better.

I would suggest this for anything. Your work friends at Christmas time. Your friend's birthdays. Meet the Teacher Night. Anything. But mainly for that damn Teacher Appreciation Week. It was a killer to any budget when my kiddos were in elementary school. I can't NOT care. That was not an option. But Mason Jars saved the day.

Buy a Dish Rack

When I used to clean houses to make ends meet way back when the kiddos were little, I cleaned for a woman who had two dishwashers. She had four kids and was always doing dishes. In her giant kitchen, in the home she designed, she made room for two dishwashers. It was a brilliant stroke of design genius for a large family. I thought to myself, "If I am ever in this situation of having loads of money, I will totally have two dishwashers."

Welp. The situation of having loads of money never actually arrived. And I have a regular kitchen with one dishwasher. But I still have mountains of dishes because we pretty much cook every meal at home, and we have loads of eaters. Dishes are everywhere at the end of a meal. Even after we load the dishwasher, there is still a sink full. About 10 years ago we came up with a solution: the simple old school dish rack.

I may have bought it at Costco or on Amazon, but it's an old school dish rack that sits on my counter next to my kitchen sink. There is typically a sink full of dishes in the sink soaking, dishes in the rack drying and dishes in the dishwasher too. But they are all on their way to clean instead of sitting in my sink filthy. I buy cheap dish soap and have a sink full of sudsy dishes ready for the drying rack. It just makes the movement of dishes from dirty to clean take place faster. And that matters when you need spoons all the time.

This past year I bought two drying mats from the grocery store. I had seen them in one of the aisles, and finally made the purchase. This allows for even more dishes to get clean and dry, and I just fold the mats when I am finished and throw them under the sink. This is now just part of my day for the movement of dishes. And there are a million text messages a week to my kids to put dishes away when they get home. And a million more bowls available on the regular. So, let me encourage you, if anything, just buy the drying rack. Set it on your counter. Take some dish soap and make magic happen. Dirty dishes piled high in the sink make me feel anxious anyway. This is one of the easiest solutions in the universe. You're welcome.

Re-Heat the Coffee

We are coffee snobs at The Hooks House. I wish it wasn't true, but it's totally true. We don't buy expensive coffee, however. We have done years of research and found one that is both inexpensive and delightful (check out Cafe Bustello if you ever get a chance). And now in our home we have four daily multi-cup coffee drinkers. Coffee goes quick. Brewing multiple pots every single morning.

But there is always that one last pot. The one that is left over, and not completely finished. The one that might sit there for a bit…or until the next morning. If you must, put it in the fridge for iced coffee later. You will thank yourself for that one little step.

If you are 900% lazy like me, just let it sit for one day. And re-heat it the next morning. I don't really care what your thoughts are on coffee sitting in a pot for a day. I don't really care if I might get a disease or something horrible…What I care about is waking up the next morning, pouring leftover coffee in a mug and heating it in the microwave for exactly 1 minute.

This may seem trite, but it really does make our coffee last longer. I mean, all leftovers make food last longer. And coffee is no exception. When you are working to make things stretch, don't stop with coffee. I have my travel mugs I bring it to work in everyday too…No need to stop and get coffee on the way…I can bring my own. And I can totally tell the difference between a re-heated cup and a fresh cup. I just don't care much at 4AM. It's caffeine and buys me just enough energy to make the pot for the morning.

Teach your family to drink re-heated coffee. You WILL thank me for this. I promise.

"Buy Nothing" Pages on Facebook

I am not sure when the Buy Nothing Community Pages came about, but they have been a lifesaver for our family for sure. These are simple pages/groups on Facebook of people in your community who have things they no longer want or need, and people who have "wishes" they are hoping to have answered by the folks in the Buy Nothing Community. Our local Buy Nothing page is amazing. I have given away random items and furniture and rugs on these pages, but what I have received has been even better!

I have furnished my children's bedrooms completely through this community...beds, dressers, mirrors, artwork, tables...the list goes on and on. And when I walk in their bedrooms, I honestly think of how lucky I am to have this community. There are often people giving away food they don't want like the woman who owns a vending machine company in my community and gave my family multiple enormous boxes of chips. Just the other day I got two cans of pumpkin which I will gladly use to make my Joshua some pumpkin bread. Or the time someone was giving away close to a million (ok that number might be high) ponytail holders...and we had like three stretched out old ones and I always forget to buy new ones. Or the awesome red shoes I picked up...I could go on forever...

But it's also the fact you get to give stuff away. Seriously. It feels good to clean out your pantry or a random closet and make someone's day. Party decorations. Clothes. A random assortment of empty bottles I had been keeping for something I can't remember...And it builds this little sharing community. We get to know each other's names and make funny comments when folks are getting rid of strange items. It's people who might live just a street or two over from you, and y'all are helping each other. It's amazing. Just search up Buy Nothing with your city/town name on Facebook and see what pops up...If there isn't anything, maybe you should start one...It's totally worth it.

Today I am going to go pick up a CD player from a gal I have never met for Grace who has become obsessed with "vintage" music. She saw that I wanted one on a different post and grabbed one for my girl and messaged me. She's also the free chips lady so there is another 5 boxes of variety chips on her porch too because she knows I have a million teens in my house. It's a reminder that neighbors still help neighbors, and kindness is sometimes literally next door.

Half Priced Books

We have sold so many items to Half Priced Books. I recently had my oldest clean out his books. After all the other kiddos going through his bags of books, I took them to Half Priced Books and got $33 cash. You can also use it for store credit. And the store credit portion was something we used all the time when my kids were little. We would take in old, gently used books and sell them back to buy new books. It was a nice little treat when you have kiddos and not a lot of money.

After a few years of moving two large boxes of cds from city to city and house to house, we finally came to the conclusion we were never going to unpack them, and they were pretty much random boxes we hauled everywhere which is just weird. We took them little by little to Half Priced Books and made some cash. We called it our football ticket cash because we used it for all the dang entry fees to a million middle school and high school games. It was just money sitting in a box in my opinion. And it was worth the trek to Half Priced Books with a bag and a little time waiting in the store as the only price I paid.

Don't forget that Half Priced Books will take puzzles and games too. They will buy back your DVD collection you can never use because you now have no DVD player. I even think they have a section for VHS tapes and cassette tapes and definitely vinyl. And it is a great little place to shop too for a million stocking stuffers or just presents in general...or books...oh my gosh the books are endless.

Get your people to do a little room clean out. Consider it the world's easiest garage sale, and head on over to your local Half Priced Book store. It is worth it. I promise.

Draco Tinkle and Twinkle Face

Ok. Let me be frank and honest here. When I was about 25 years old, one of my students asked me why I had a mustache. Ever since then I have been waxing, tweezing and threading my upper lip and eyebrows chasing that baby smooth I had in my youth. It has been done by friends and done in salons...I have spent upwards of $30 and as little as $15...Love when I had someone to do it for free, but that is like lightning in a bottle.

Recently, I was at a party in Houston and my dear friend, Jody, handed me two Twinkle Face "shavers". Folks. I went home and gave it a shot and it has been a month since I have done anything to my upper lip or my eyebrows. They are $15 for 60 on Amazon. What???? This means you are paying pennies to get your "lady stache" taken care of and no time at the random nail place in the back room.

And when I posted about this very item, so many people already knew about Twinkle Face and had been using it for YEARS. How did I miss this very awesome boat? I have friends who do their whole face because it makes you look younger. I have a friend who uses it on her toes…yes…these are the things we seldom talk about. I have friends who heard about it from their grandmas…Again…how did I miss this???

But the bottom line is…you're spending barely any money and taking almost zero time out of your schedule. I cannot say this enough. There are products that are beyond worth it and this is just one of them. Do yourself a favor and jump on Amazon and place your order. I have zero shame when it comes to keeping my lip free of hair. So, join me in saving some money. You will be so thankful you did.

WL Intimates (My six pack of bras)

So, I had gotten to the point in my life where my bras were falling apart. I mean like underwires sticking out. Holes. They didn't fit anymore either. And there was nothing I could do. I could buy a bra here and there but, even bras at Target are $20 or more each. There was no way I could go back to the days of Victoria's Secret or go get sized for a bra or spend anything other than Monopoly money…I have four kids…they need underwear…constantly…and my girl needs bras…It just had started to feel like my lot in life. I was to wear bras from 1982 and have my boobs hit my waistline on a daily basis. Not really what I want for myself.

HOWEVER, during Covid when I had 9 million hours a day to scroll through Amazon to find a deal, I discovered WL Intimates. Y'all. This is my six pack of bras. They come in all sorts of colors and sizes too. But the best part is that it's a damn six pack of bras and the MOST I have ever seen them sell for is $33. You can't beat this price. You just can't. And they are good bras too. Full of support which is what I need after 47 years of life.

It was my treat to myself one payday. And it made me feel so much better about myself. I felt younger and as strange as this may sound, I felt like I mattered. I have suggested this same purchase to anyone who will listen to me…I know there are so many of us with threadbare bras on our body…I remember my mom being the same way with her bras falling apart…And yes, in the grand scheme of life, I am certain bras don't matter, but it mattered to me. And it felt good to get a multicolored six pack of cutie pie bras in the mail. Just treat yourself. You will be so glad you did.

Sun Burnt

We are sunshine folks in The Hooks House. We live in Texas, and we have to be in the pool or a body of water the moment it gets hot which is like March. We have used a million Aloe Vera treatments for sun burns, but there is only one I swear by…Sun Burnt. We order it on Amazon at the beginning of Spring Break and then continue to order it as it runs out through the rest of the 22-month summers here in The Lone Star State. It has more than just aloe in it, and I think this is part of the reason it works so well.

I tell my kiddos to slather it on their sunburns and it always finds a way to turn into some golden-brown skin. I have never been disappointed. And I am not lying when I tell you we have used every product over the years, and this is the one I have picked as my "go to". Get yourself a bottle or a tube…especially if you're heading to the beach or a water park. You will thank me later.

Donate Plasma

If you can, you should totally consider donating plasma. It is something we discovered from a friend who had been donating plasma for years. Yes, it is a bit of a commitment…Think maybe three hours a week, but you get paid. And you get paid pretty well for a few hours a week while you have the plasma removed from your blood. You will have to complete a physical once a year and do vitals every time you are at the plasma donation site. Yes, you will have to juggle it already into your super tight schedule, but it has been a lifesaver for us and the friends of ours who also are on the donation rotation.

We have donated (both Corey and I donate) to pay for vacations. We have donated for extra cash and to pay for all the incidentals. I have friends who donates for their kiddos' Christmas presents, or for their once-a-year family trip. We have donated to help pay for Senior pictures and all the Senior year of high school things. We have donated for gas money at this stage in life. And we have donated for the extra $100 it gives us a week.

Truth be told, every single time I donate I meet another teacher. Clearly that should be noted somewhere. I have run into friends and other parents. I have learned people I love have donated plasma for years because it is just the extra money you might need for the extra thing you are paying for…I have a friend who donates for her car payment each month. And I believe if you asked all of us who donate, it is 100% worth it. There is always something a little extra cash can help. And I believe we are all brilliant for finding a way to keep our life going. Some of us don't have time for the extra part time job, but we could have time to donate a little plasma. Check it out. Find a donation center near you and give it a shot. This might be the boost your bank account has been looking for all this time.

Pictures and Song Lyrics for Presents

Sometimes buying presents can be the most stressful part of any season…Christmas…birthdays…Mother's Day…you name it…Giving presents to people you adore especially when you are pinching every last penny, can feel like a shame spiral. I want you to know that some of the most meaningful presents I have received were cell phone pictures blown up and put in frames or the lyrics of a song printed out and framed. You can't go wrong with this…It is one of the best gifts to give anytime.

I have friends who I have printed some selfies we took and put them in frames, and they loved it! And these frames can be regular, inexpensive frames from Dollar General or Walmart. They can be a pack of five you bought off Amazon and keep them in your closet. I have blown up cute pictures of my sons and their girlfriends to give for Valentine's Day. And it takes no time at all to run to your local CVS or Walgreen's or Walmart photo. These days you can hook your phone right up to the machine at most places…no fuss at all.

The song lyrics take a little more time, but not a lot. It's the lyrics to their favorite song or the lyrics to "your song". It's the one that will get hung in a room or a hallway to remind you when someone hears that song, they instantly think of you. My best friend gave me the lyrics to "Rainbow Connection" in a frame years ago, and I cried when I opened it. One year my sister gave Grace the lyrics to a "Dear Evan Hanson" song in a frame, and it still sits out on her dresser. It really is one of the most sentimental gifts…and it's easy…

So, don't overthink life too much. Don't make it more complicated than it already is these days. Don't think the more you spend, the more they will love it. Sometimes it is that candid shot on your camera roll, or the lyrics to the song you used to scream at the top of your lungs from a million days gone by. Trust me. Pictures and song lyrics. It will be the gift they keep with them for a long, long time.

Cafe Bustelo

My husband and I are serious coffee snobs. We have tried to not care so much, but we care SO MUCH. We love rich and expensive coffee. I mean, we seriously love overpriced coffee and have such a hard time if we have crappy coffee. We are ridiculous about it especially when we live on a tight budget. So, we have been on a mission to make this all work out for our mornings. We are not two cups a day coffee drinkers. We are the folks that drink coffee all day long.

We discovered Cafe Bustelo a couple of years ago. It is so inexpensive, and it tastes so good. It is rich and bold and full of yumminess. We spend less than $6 on a can, and if we buy the brick of coffee, it costs even less. And our mornings are full of the coffee we love at the price we can totally get behind.

You can buy Cafe Bustelo on Amazon, or at Walmart or even Dollar General. Strong and lovely. Thank you to my Dad for drinking it forever…We finally took note.

Glow Necklaces at Every Party

I used to stress over favors for birthday parties. I really did. Younger me was always stressed. But as years have gone on and on, I am pretty certain I am not going to spend my money on a bag of little random crap toys…So, I usually just have glow necklaces. Everyone loves a glow necklace. Adults and kids alike. There is just something about a glow necklace that makes a party a little more partyish…A little more fun…Trust me on this one.

The other big fun thing is to let kids submit their five picks for the party playlist. They love it when their songs come on. It never gets old to hear the song you picked at a party. It's the twenty first century version of "Requests and Dedications". They will all sing along too.

I am serious when I say, glow necklaces and have your guests submit their songs for the party playlist...super simple, but can make all the difference.

Two Loads of Laundry a Day

I do not have time to have an official laundry day. There is about zero ways I could make that happen. So, I do two loads of laundry a day. Hear me now when I say that I don't put two loads of laundry away a day. But I do wash and dry them. Yes. Sometimes it is more than two. However, because I typically do two loads of laundry a day, there is always at least one day that I do NO loads of laundry. Pretty great.

Laundry with four kids can seem like the bane of your existence. Two loads a day seems manageable. I usually do them both before I leave for work since I wake up so dang early, however, you do you. If you are up late or if you work from home or if you do them the moment you get home from work...it doesn't matter...Just two seemed super manageable to me...And so this is my system.

This honestly is just about saving your brain power for other things...saving choices and time and your thoughts and such for the things that truly matter. Laundry does not matter. It just has to get done. Folded and put away is for someone else's book...I haven't gotten there yet.

Buy the Block of Cheese

It's just cheaper. Honestly. I buy a block of Medium Cheddar each week I go to the grocery store. I shred it if I need to for things like tacos or burritos or enchiladas or nachos. I slice it thin for sandwiches. I cut it up for cheese and crackers. But it just lasts longer and ends up being cheaper. I used to buy the sliced cheese for the sandwiches and the shredded cheese for anything else. But a block of cheese each week seems to answer it all. And when you are pinching pennies, like we often are around here, a block of cheese is worth it. Trust me. Buy the block of cheese.

Ask for the Discount

My kids have gotten used to it…I'm going to ask for the discount. So many places have discounts they don't tell you about upfront. All you have to do is ask. I ask for a teacher discount and a student discount now that I have a college student…If he's with me this always helps. There are a bunch of places with First Responder discounts too. And don't forget a military discount or a veteran discount. They are out there, and they are everywhere. Movie theaters, restaurants, clothing stores, bookstores…All you have to do is ask.

I have taught my kiddos this too, and my oldest was shocked at the student discount recently when he went to the movies…not just on his ticket, but on the snacks too. It made a huge difference. And remember, lots of stores will offer teacher discounts in the summer months. You can always google what stores offer discounts and I promise, you will be pleasantly surprised. All you have to do is ask. And I am never ashamed to ask for a discount.

Even if it's just one roll, Keep the Leftover

I will keep one roll in a Ziplock bag if it's leftover. I will keep a small portion of scrambled eggs, mashed potatoes, one tortilla, a shred of shredded cheese…if it's leftover I'm probably keeping it…The reason being is simple, it WILL get eaten.

I will reheat scrambled eggs for someone's breakfast the next day. I have watched a roll become a "fancy" sandwich in someone's lunchbox and the random sparse amount of shredded cheddar creates a one-man quesadilla. We have far too many people in this house to let anything go to waste. And I encourage my kids and husband to find what they can in the fridge when they are hunting for food. Today my daughter ate the small container of mashed potatoes left in the fridge…It's what's for lunch or breakfast the next day that counts when it comes to leftovers.

Invite People Over for Dinner

I used to think inviting people over had to be fancy…Like I had to have some special sort of meal to have my friends over. But as times got leaner and leaner and going out was not an option, having people over became the answer.

I want to tell you that people will happily eat chicken nuggets and macaroni and cheese if you put it on a plate before them. They will eat grilled cheese, frozen pizza, corn dogs...anything...if you put it on a plate in front of them. They are there for your company...not for your fancy. And to be honest with you, when you invite people into your ordinary home with zero frills, it gives them permission to be themselves...And it gives them permission to have people over too. Nachos are a good one too...Everyone loves nachos. Just don't be afraid to ask them over and save all that money on tipping a waiter...Sit on your back porch or your couch or just stand around the kitchen...handing out realness by the bucketful. It matters so much more than a centerpiece and a five-course meal.

And remember this, I always remind myself, if I am feeling lonely, someone else is feeling lonely too. Invite people over. You've got nothing to lose.

Re-Gifting is Really Real

We all receive random gifts we are not going to use...or that don't really fit our personality...or that we just don't like. And it is ok. As gift givers we swing, and we miss. As humans I believe it is 900% worth it to have a regift stash in your house...mine is in a closet...and it is where all the gifts live that are awesome...but just not meant for me...I am going to regift them. I am going to be in a bind and need a present and have no cash, and I am going to regift something. And I am going to believe the new recipient will love it so much more.

I feel no shame in this…I am giving a gift new life. And I am not breaking my bank account for all the countless gifts I may all of a sudden have to hand out. It is what it is. And I highly suggest you let go of the guilt (if you have any) and begin to regift the things you are never going to use.

15 Minutes of Fame Parties

I am not sure if this company is nationwide or just in Texas, but it is amazing. These are some of the best family photos we have ever taken for the least amount of money. You can search them up on Facebook or Google it. You simply sign up for a party and drag your whole family in color coordinated clothes and then spend 15 minutes in front of a professional photographer.

It's all you get. And for some reason, the 15-minute time limit is all you need. You laugh. You're in a hurry. You are in and out of there in 15 minutes and your entire family can handle it. I can tell you it is also cost effective. We always order every digital print and then make all of our canvases or Christmas presents or hallway hangings at Walmart or CVS or Walgreens…whatever has the biggest and best coupon. Take a minute and see if there is one in your area…if not, throw your own 15 Minutes of Fame Party and invite your friends. We did this once and received all of our photos for free. Totally worth it.

And I will say it again, these are some of the best family photos we have ever taken hands down. And who doesn't have 15 minutes to spare?

Angel Milk

We made this up a million years ago I think…maybe someone told us about it…I can't know…

A warm cup of milk with a teaspoon of vanilla in it. We have given it to our kiddos when they are having trouble sleeping…I told them it helps you sleep…maybe it does…it seems to make them feel better…And it's easy and warm and delicious.

And they always go to bed after. It feels like magic parenting gold.

The Tube of Meat

Y'all. We buy the tube of hamburger meat. So many people may disagree with this, but it is just less expensive and when you are making sure 6 people eat, welp, you can't be embarrassed to grab it at the store. It's just the same as the Styrofoam meat…maybe not…I can't know…I'm certain of one thing though, the packaging saves you considerable money…And that is just what it is about for me sometimes.

I had someone give me a big speech about upgrading to the Styrofoam meat. I felt really bad about myself afterwards, and I thought I was a bad mom. Like, literally, thought I was a bad mom. But I can tell you I have had some of the best conversations with the other folks grabbing the tube of meat too. We seem like a real fine lot of cost cutting humans. And I just can't care anymore about what some old friend felt the need to tell me when they are clearly not walking a mile in my shoes.

So, hold your head up high. Buy the damn tube of meat and save the money. Live on my friends.

Road Trip Bathrooms

I had three kids potty training for what seemed like a billion years. It was horrible. I had three 3 and under too for a point of time, and that was a fuckton of diapers. I was a well-traveled critic of the public restroom. I spent a ton of time in them. On top of this, we were also the family who was and is driving to see grandparents. Sometimes a 12-hour drive with me and potty training or diapered kiddos. It felt like the most horribly hard situation taking children into public restrooms especially on road trips. But I learned a few things and mapped my route accordingly for years upon years. Now that they are 19, 17, 16 and 10 it is a different story all together…I mean shoot…I have extra drivers on road trips…But back in the day I literally decided my stops and my route based on one thing: BATHROOMS.

You can always count on Buc-ee's. It is like the Mecca of bathrooms and cleanliness and snacks and kolaches and shopping galore. Their mascot is a beaver, and their marketing is impeccable. If you see a Buc-ee's on a road trip with or without children just go ahead and stop. It is always worth it. It is always enjoyable. And you will thank yourself for the much-needed happy break you took while driving in the car with people you may grow to hate and possibly want to kill over the next many hours. The Buc-ee's stop will ease any fighting in the car between your family members and go ahead and buy the Beaver Nuggets…and a shirt…or heck, just stop for the best bathrooms ever and a smile. This is my number one road trip bathroom suggestion. However, Buc-ee's is not in every state, and it's not on every route. You have to have a few more tricks up your sleeve especially when traveling with children.

Starbucks restrooms are always immaculate. Often, they are private bathrooms too with lots of room to crowd multiple children into and have them all wait patiently. This was my life during the days of road trips solo with children. I had to take them all into the bathroom with me because they were little…or I was changing a diaper and wanted the cleanest space available to put my baby on…Starbucks is tried and true in the restroom department. And there are a million Starbucks across the planet so, I could usually find one along the way.

Chick Fil A is tip top for cleanliness and kind employees…bonus for the playscape your kiddos can get out energy running and climbing and screaming their head off during your stops. The service is amazing and other parents are there feeling your pain. And the bathrooms are glorious. I have a couple of times tried stopping at a different fast-food chain and was horribly disappointed. The one downside is if you are traveling on a Sunday you have to have a different option.

Target bathrooms are one of my top choices too. I can get all my kiddos into a Target bathroom and know they will be clean, and their staff is pretty friendly too. When we stop at Target, we grab snacks and we are on our way. But the bathrooms were what drew us in on many a road trip. And bathrooms matter to me a lot.

I always try to prepare myself to stop often on road trips. I try to prepare myself for the one kid who will need to "go" right after we pull away from the house or the Starbucks. I have done my best to keep them on track with one of these fine establishments on the horizon. But I will tell you, we have stopped at some sketch places numerous times, and I cannot hate it enough. If you can, get to that Buc-Ee's, Starbucks, Chick Fil A or Target to potty. You will thank yourself. I promise.

Ornaments and Coffee Mugs

We are weirdos with odd little traditions, but they work. Each of my kiddos is a "bear", and they have that bear imprinted on their hearts...or at least brainwashed into their brains. Jake is an American Brown Bear. Jude is a Polar Bear. Grace is a Koala Bear (yes...I know it's a marsupial...I didn't know that at the time though). Josh is a Panda Bear. For Christmas each year they get an ornament of their bear. Just an easy little gift in their stocking. And now our tree is filled with bears...and koala bears...galore.

We also drink water out of coffee mugs in the morning. I do not know why we do this. I have no logic or reason behind it. Every year each kiddo gets a coffee mug in their stocking too. I try to find ones that fit their personality or have a character on them they love. This year Grace got yet another David Bowie mug (I didn't realize there were so many made), Jude and Josh got ones from Sesame Street and Jake got one with the middle finger on it...perfect for my college kid.

For some reason these are the little traditions that they look forward to...No, it's not their favorite present, but it's a family tradition and those things are what you can count on even if the world is screwy. They get excited about them and know they are going to be waiting in their stockings and they always want to see who got what...

These are little not so little things you can do to build some traditions in your homes. And they count more than you know. It matters. The tiny details. They matter. The things that whisper, "I thought of you." Those are the things that matter.

Bedsure Blankets as Graduation Gifts

My son, Jake, received a Bedsure fleece blanket monogrammed with his initials and OU for a graduation present. And it was the softest blanket in the universe. This has become my standard graduation present: a fleece Bedsure blanket in their school colors monogrammed with their initials and the logo of the school. I order them on Amazon, and they are NOT expensive. I actually have a friend who monograms for me...But as a mom who has year after year of graduates in her life (I am in the throes of kiddos graduating) this is my go to.

I know what I am getting every single graduate on my list, and it is not a super expensive gift…but it is a GREAT blanket. I have heard from most of the kids I bought them for last year that it was their absolute favorite.

Take the stress out of buying for graduates. Have your standard present ready to go and order on Amazon. Easy peasy. And whether it's for a graduation gift or not, I am here to tell you Bedsure blankets are the best blankets hands down and they cost less than $20.

Gift Someone A Playlist

When my son, Jake, was about to go away to college, we all added songs to a Spotify playlist titled, The Bear. There were funny songs added we had laughed at as a family. Songs we thought were important for him to hear and know. Songs that meant something to us. Songs that made us think of him. And each of us added tons. Our goal was to make the playlist as long as his drive from Norman, OK to Buda, TX. It's about 7 hours. And y'all, it's the best playlist. This was such a sentimental thing to do. And Jake loved it. It's like the soundtrack of his life at home. I still add songs to it every once in a while. This was one of the cheapest and easiest things I have ever done as a gift…And it was lovely. I highly suggest you do this for people you love…The result was amazing.

Bottle to Bottle

Most of us are willing to turn over shampoo bottles in our shower to eek out the end of the contents to get one or two more rinses. But I want you to know this works for other liquids too. In my house if there are two bottles of syrup and one is almost empty, I combine them. Same with liquid hand soap or honey…the thick liquids. I open the bottles, place one right side up and the other is balanced on top to let the liquid run out. In the end it makes one full bottle. It may sound trite, but every little bit helps and throwing things out is just not an option for The Hooks Family. Every ounce of syrup will get used if it's just in one full bottle.

Pack Your Lunch and Snacks

I pack my lunch every day for work. And a bag of snacks. I am not meal prepping to be healthy, I'm just packing a lunch to save money. All of the trips to a restaurant are grand, but I simply can't afford it. I don't want to spend my money that way anyways. So, I pack a lunch and a bag of snacks and some drinks too. I have a refrigerator and microwave in my classroom which helps a lot. This doesn't mean I don't leave and take a lunch break…It just means most days I save money by eating at my desk. And I'm not starving all day either because I bring everything from nuts and fruit to random leftovers from my house…

Easy Dinner Night

OK. Everything I make is pretty easy, however, I put one easy easy dinner on the menu each week. This means I am going to stick something in the oven, or have a no thought, barely any prep time meal. There is a basic rotation for this too:

Hot Dogs and Mac-N-Cheese
Corn Dogs and Mac-N-Cheese
Chicken Nuggets and Mac-N-Cheese
Frozen Pizzas

Those are the options. Nothing fancy. Just no thought at all required. And everyone always loves it like it's the best night of the week. I mean, it's kid food. And who doesn't like a little bit of kid food. Chicken nuggets are honestly divine.

Bob Books

Bob Books have been around forever. I received a set of them from my Stepmom, Maureen, when Jake was about 4 years old. She swore by them. And we used that same set to teach all four kids how to read. They are these tiny 1970's era early early reading books. They have my favorite artwork in them ever. And they build such confidence in new readers. I am never letting them go. I recently loaned them out to a friend who had a child who was a late reader and struggling and therefore avoided reading. She loved them as much as I did because they build confidence…I'm telling you, moms in the 1970's knew what they were doing...I believe you can still order the complete set on Amazon. If you are teaching littles to read, this is one of the world's greatest purchases.

Write Love Notes

Everyone loves a love note. They are simple and free. They are pieces of paper with love written down. You took the time to write your love on a piece of paper...it's what makes it a big deal. I still write them to my people. I cut out heart shapes and write love notes. I just tucked one into a box headed for The University of Oklahoma where my Bear lives. I just wrote two recently for my January birthday kiddos. And they are always needed. Put a love note in your partner's driver seat. Put a love note next to their bed. Love notes in lunchboxes forever. In the hands of the menacing Elf on the Shelf. At the breakfast table. Inside backpacks and suitcases. This is a little piece of your heart for someone else. Love notes matter. I promise.

Let Them Paint with Water

When my kiddos were toddlers, I would get them a big, big bucket of water and some paintbrushes you might use to pain a house...I would stick them out in the backyard by the fence or by the house and let them "paint" everything. This was a summertime activity because the water would dry super-fast, and they could watch it dry and then paint it again. This might take up huge chunks of a hot afternoon. And I was such a cool mom because I let them "paint" the house or the fence or the playhouse. I even let them "paint" each other. How cool am I? I have passed this tip on to countless young parents...It is really the activity that just keeps on giving...

When they finally put down the brushes to come inside, the fence and house are a little cleaner...And maybe those kids are too. No harm in "painting" your little brother or sister with a massive amount of water.

College Boxes

There is a group of us who had kiddos all graduate and head to college at the same time...I'm sure there are lots of parents in the same situation. One day our dear friend, Claire Bear, decided to gather all the kids' addresses, put the names in a hat and draw a name for each month for the lot of us. Each month we have a different kiddo (who is not our own kiddo), and we send them a little box in the mail.

Y'all. This is one of the best and most fun ideas ever. You pack the kid's favorite snacks, maybe a gift card, coffee, funny items (I have sent lots of Bedsure blankets with monogrammed initials or sorority/fraternity letters), a cute note, socks, treats...you name it. And it is just a reminder for your college students that they are loved. It takes a little time to plan it out and make it to the post office, but there is nothing better than getting a text or call from a kiddo you haven't seen in quite some time knowing they got a surprise delivery. It warms your heart.

So, get with a group of friends…not a huge group…There are five of us and it works great…Just make it happen…exchange addresses and draw names. It makes you feel good as a mom too knowing once a month your kid will feel the love from someone else who loves them too. And what isn't better than happy mail? Pick the friends. Send the boxes. Feel the love.

Frozen Things in the Crockpot

When I was 35, my husband lived in Houston, and I lived in Arlington with three little kids and worked full time as a high school teacher. High School began at 7:15 and getting everyone to the right place felt brutal at times. And dinner. How the hell was I going to get dinner on the table when all the crockpot recipes called for 6 to 8 hours on low…or 4 hours…And I was gone some days for 12 hours straight. It felt so frustrating. Until I learned one of the best secrets ever…You can put frozen meat in the crockpot and let it cook all day.

I would put frozen chicken, cream of mushroom soup and rice in a crockpot at 5:30AM, and by 6PM it was all perfectly cooked. No need to worry. I could still make the same recipes.

Please use this tip. Just put it in frozen and cook it on low if your days look more like 12 hours gone by the time you're home from practices too. It was a lifesaver for me and my family. I hope it is for you and yours too.

Get 2 Liters for Parties

This might sound really silly but get the 2-liter bottles of soda for parties. I used to buy a six pack or a 12 pack and would wind up picking up a million cans with two sips out of each. Kids would take two sips, set it down, lose track of it and grab another can. Oh, my word, how frustrating and wasteful. However, if you get the two liters and some cheap plastic cups (Red Solo cups are for the fancy parties) you can just make it last longer...all the sodas. Hand out the sharpie for the kiddos to mark their cup territory and your drinks just might last till the last person leaves. Besides, 2 liters are always on sale. You'll thank me for this the next time a pack of 11-year-olds eats you out of house and home.

Stay Up As Late As You Want

We have had a rule with all of our kiddos and it has worked like a charm with each and every one. You are allowed to stay up as late as you want under one condition...you have to be reading. We have equipped all of our kiddos with head lamps at one time or another. And honestly, they can throw caution to the wind if they are reading a book...magazine...comic book...And it has helped to create kids who will read.

It's exciting when you're in elementary school if you can have that crazy permission to put on a head lamp and read till you fall asleep. And they will always fall asleep. But man, they feel so grown up finishing a chapter or five after bedtime. Make this rule especially if you have a kid who does NOT like to read. The promise of no curfew if they are reading. And reading is like gold.

Solving Stinky Feet

All four of my kiddos went through this weird and horrible stinky feet phase. It happens somewhere around 1st and 2nd grade and it's horrendous. Like clearing a room bad. And the first three we just kind of suffered through it. Washing shoes. Trying all sorts of odor eaters. Mandating socks. Dying. You name it. But with Josh when he hit this phase my friend, Sheena gave us the cure. 1 cup white vinegar in a big bowl or bucket of warm water to soak the stinky feet in for 15 minutes.

And it works. We were doing it once a week for a while with Josh because that is what was needed, and slowly but surely, we soaked less and less feet. And now we are passed the stage. Could have saved myself so many, "Oh my God! Jesus! Put your shoes back on!!!" While driving a minivan.

Fake Ice Cubes

Years and years ago my mom bought us a package of fake ice cubes. We were really not impressed by this but held on to them just the same. However, summertime rolled around, and we were packing a million coolers to go to a million pools or water parks. Every single time the fake ice cubes felt like a lifesaver. You just put them in your cooler like regular ice and holy smokes...they work. No big cooler of leftover water at the end of the day either. And you just take them home and re-freeze them. I just brought them with us to the beach so we could pack our little day cooler of tequila and soda water to sit on the beach. I use regular ice packs too instead of buying the big bags of ice. Can't help but think it's saving us a little money here and there and a bit of a headache too. We have been using this system for what seems like forever, and I will never ever go back.

The Lego Sheet

We have accumulated a big bin of Lego's over the years with four kiddos. And when the kids were little, they would dump them out and it would drive me absolutely crazy. All those Legos all over the floor. Picking them up was a beast. Then one day I had a brilliant idea that I am certain someone else gave to me...Because really...all our brilliant ideas come from other moms and dads...I got a regular flat sheet and laid it on the floor. Dumped the bin of Legos on the sheet. And they played and played. When they were done, I scooped up the Lego sheet by the four corners and placed it back in the bin.

This became essential to Lego fun. I could put the sheet in the front yard and dump Legos and they would all come back easy peasy. I could take it to a friend's house this way or wherever. And it was just a twin sized regular old sheet saving the day again and again. Hope this helps someone out there just a little bitty bit. Grab the sheet. It's so worth it.

Costco Vacations

We don't have a lot of vacation money, but a few years ago we had friends tell us about Costco Vacations. They have so many options. You can go just about anywhere and yes; you have to have a Costco membership. But you can pick and build a vacation and spread out your payments for a year. It has been so worth it for us and actually our marriage. It's vacation lay away. And you just keep making your payments and dreaming of being together.

I know there is probably a cheaper way, but I also don't have a lot of time. So, someone having a million options for me and a one stop shop for payment has been lovely. No. We don't do this all the time. No. It's not something happening every year. But it HAS happened, and it will happen again someday when we don't have a million kids in college. Just know this little gem exists for you and yours and all the dreams you have in your heart of seeing a beach someday with a fancy drink in your hand. In the words of my dad, "You will never regret the trip to Aruba."

Slip On Shoes

We have a rule in our house that we enforce to this day…If we are going to be on a road trip, you MUST wear slip on shoes. These can be sandals. Flip Flops. Vans. Crocs. You name it, but you must have on slip on shoes. Because Lord knows the moment a car ride begins that will take longer than 30 minutes, all four of my children take their shoes off. And it took about two road trips for me to make this rule.

Stopping at a gas station or a restaurant or rest area and searching for shoes…tying them…lacing up boots…it was all too much for this mom to handle. So, even now that two of my children are adults…slip on shoes. And that includes me. I don't have time for anything more than you slipping your feet into the shoes in 2 seconds flat. Save yourself. Honest.

Leftover Lunch

We started leftover lunch when my kids were in elementary school. On Saturdays we would pull out every single leftover remnant of food in the fridge and pantry. We would heat it up and put it on the table. And it might be a million things…a little spaghetti noodles…some chicken noodle soup…one roll…leftover french toast…whatever…and it would be a big sit-down lunch. We did this no matter who was present too. Other neighborhood kids got to experience the crazy Saturday buffet. And it just meant nothing would go to waste. And it was funny too. And just another way to stretch the almighty dollar one more time.

All in All…

Love your people. Spend time with them. I cannot say it enough, daily time with your people is where connection comes in…Have a family group text…Make it horrible and inappropriate if needed…Make it full of cheers and celebrations…Make it where everyone can see each other when they are far away…Tell your kids you love them over texts…And keep writing them love notes. Maybe it's in their lunchbox. Maybe it's in their suitcase when they pack to leave home. Maybe it's at their cereal bowl in the morning. Write them down… the words you want to say to them. They need to know it. And that goes for your partner too…Write the words in your handwriting down and leave it for them…We all need love. There is no such thing as too much love.

And by all means, tell them out loud. Tell them all the time. Tell them every time you get off the phone and every time they walk out the door. And every time you think it when you see their beautiful faces.

And I need you to know, we cannot give The Hooks Kids huge lavish gifts. We cannot hand them hundreds of dollars and a hug. My son left to return to college the other day, and I handed him the $19 cash I had in my wallet…I got a big hug in return…I have a friend who lets her kiddo use all her Chick Fil A points…I hand my broke teens gift cards with a few dollars left on them…they can make it work like a coupon…And most of all I can give them love. And laughter. And a home where the door is always open. And they can be themself. Just who they are all the time. Because love just loves. Love is free. And it should be handed out by the bucketful.

I am crazy about my people. I am crazy about how much I want to spend every second with them. I am crazy emotional about how much they mean to me. I made a decision years ago that I would cry more about real life (happy and sad tears) than I do commercials or movies or TV shows…I want to be fully alive and fully invested with the people I come in contact with…but my people the most…the people in my circle…the people I live life with…I want to be fully alive with them. I want them to know me. I want to know them. I want to create a place and a space where you can breathe in and out. A real space. It becomes kinda holy. No. It IS a holy space.

And I quit wishing to have picture perfect people. That shit is for social media. I cannot do it. We are not striving for perfection over here…we are striving for greatness. And you are too, right? You are striving for great families. We want the type of families where our kids will be excited to come over with their own families someday. To eat food. To have a few drinks. To share us with the people they have found to love. All in all, this is what it's all about.

I hope this book has handed you some peace of mind. I hope this book has given you some new tips and tricks and a few Cheap and Easy dinners. I hope there is a rebirth of at home birthday parties and dinner table conversations in your home and leftovers in your bellies. I hope you know you're not alone in your crazy life. I hope you know we are all making horribly funny mistakes along this road. And I hope mostly you know you are good…just as you are…you are good.

Come visit The Hooks House someday. I will make you a drink and tell you the stories too insane to make it in this book. I'll give you some yummy hot mess out of a crockpot and pull you up a chair at our table. And you will leave with a smile and a hug. It's all we have to offer, but it sure feels like the very best we can give anyone. And don't try to give more. We all know this, but at the end of life it will be the feelings you felt with the people you loved that you will carry across with you. Remember this…Those feelings carry us through the hard times too. Cherish this love. Cherish it like it is the best of the best. I would be happy in a box eating hamburger helper if my people are with me. This is totally an absolute. This is the total truth.

So. Happy days to you, my friend. Happy happy days. With the people you love. Happiest of days.

Made in the USA
Coppell, TX
28 July 2023